ClipArt & Dynamic Designs
for
Libraries & Media Centers

Print Shop™ Graphics for Libraries Series

Vol. 1   *Print Shop Graphics for Libraries*
    Apple version ISBN 0-931510-17-1
    Mac version ISBN 0-931510-26-0

Vol. 2   *Print Shop Graphics for Libraries: Perpetual Calendars*
    Apple version ISBN 0-87287-606-3
    IBM version ISBN 0-87287-688-8

Vol. 3   *Print Shop Graphics for Libraries: Books and Fonts*
    Apple version ISBN 0-87287-659-4
    Mac version ISBN 0-87287-689-6

Vol. 4   *Print Shop Graphics for Libraries: Dynamic Library Graphics*
    (contains the graphics in this book)
    Apple version ISBN 0-87287-690-X
    Mac version ISBN 0-87287-691-8

ClipArt & Dynamic Designs
for
Libraries & Media Centers
Volume 1: Books & Basics

Judy Gay Matthews
Michael Mancarella
Shirley Lambert

1988
LIBRARIES UNLIMITED, INC.
Englewood, Colorado

LIBRARIES UNLIMITED, INC.
P.O. Box 3988
Englewood, CO 80155-3988

Matthews, Judy Gay.
    ClipArt & dynamic designs for libraries & media
centers.

    Bibliography: v. 1, p. 181.
    Includes index.
    Contents: v.1. Books & basics.
    1. Library publications--Handbooks, manuals, etc.
2. Libraries and publishing--Handbooks, manuals, etc.
3. Copy art--Handbooks, manuals, etc.
4. Books in art--Handbooks, manuals, etc.
5. Libraries in art--Handbooks, manuals, etc.
6. Copying processes--Handbooks, manuals, etc.
I. Mancarella, Michael. II. Lambert, Shirley.
III. Title. IV. Title: ClipArt and dynamic designs
for libraries & media centers. V. Title: Clip art
& dynamic designs for libraries' media centers.
Z716.6.M36 1988   686.2'24   87-33877
ISBN 0-87287-636-5 (v. 1)

Contents

v

**Part 2
CLIP ART**

Preface

This is a book of clip art and graphic techniques designed for librarians, teachers, story-tellers, and other people interested in books and libraries. Its purpose is to assist in the creation of printed products such as flyers, newsletters, announcements, bookmarks, lettering for displays, bulletin boards, and other forms of visual communication.

In examining other books of clip art on the market, the authors have found very little that is intended specifically for the library. Books of general clip art include art that libraries can use, such as holiday pictures, pictures of children, and pictures on contemporary topics, but very little on BOOKS. In creating announcements for the books which Libraries Unlimited publishes, the authors have found very little clip art which could be applied to book topics; we have produced this book, therefore, for public librarians, school media specialists, business and technical librarians, university and college librarians, bookstores, and even other publishing companies.

The first part of the book contains practical suggestions for the novice about the creation of graphic and printed products. This section discusses techniques, materials, and equipment, and provides a number of suggestions to make the product attractive and professional looking. The authors have tried to present some general guidelines in each section, rather than concentrating on technical and theoretical aspects. Terms in boldface can be found in the Glossary. Each chapter will take you step-by-step and give you tips for saving time and for producing a professional piece using materials which are easy to obtain. Sample costs are frequently included.

If you know absolutely nothing about using clip art, the introductory material will be essential for you. If you are a seasoned professional, you will be more interested in the art itself, and you will find a great variety from which to choose. Included are geometric and repetitive designs, pictures of children, books, calendar graphics, designs for library events, cartoons, and photographic effects.

In part 2, a section entitled "Very Simple Projects" incorporates some of the drawings, borders, and folding ideas. This section demonstrates how to combine several images; create a sleek, up-beat mood; and cut, clip, or trim art for a dramatic effect or better fit. These concepts are intended as a springboard. Reshape the designs, add to them, allow them to stimulate your imagination, and transform your ideas into a visual message with impact.

Finally, we have included a collection of clip art which can be copied, photographed, traced, or otherwise used in printed products. A particular effort has been made to include pictures of books in many positions and situations, with enough space to label them in a flyer or announcement. Illustrations are simple, with bold ink lines; they will reproduce well, even on a photocopier. As long as your products are not for resale, you may use any illustration as is or modify it in any way you like. If you are producing a publication which will be sold (such as a history of your local library), you may also use this clip art. It is only if you are producing a book of designs for sale (such as a coloring book) which incorporates the designs in this book, in whole or in part, that permission for use must be sought. Reselling these pictures as clip art is, of course, prohibited.

For the Computer Crowd

Many of the designs in this book are also available on computer disk, either for the MacIntosh (order *Dynamic Library Graphics*, Mac version, ISBN 0-87287-691-8) or for the Apple (order *Dynamic Library Graphics*, Apple version, ISBN 0-87287-690-X). Both are available from Libraries Unlimited.

Acknowledgments

The authors would like to thank each of the illustrators who contributed his or her creative efforts to this book. Their addresses are on file at Libraries Unlimited—they are all freelancers who accept outside jobs, and they are all a pleasure to work with.

Maria Crow, who lives in Littleton, Colorado, is the resident artist/cameraperson at South Park Graphics, a printing and design company in Littleton. Her expertise in illustrating was acquired on her own and in coursework at Abilene Christian University, Texas.

Darcie Frohardt lives in Denver and currently teaches drawing to three-, four-, and five-year-olds. Her illustration skills are basically self-taught. She has a strong background in crafts and craft media of all kinds, a love of books and reading, and a MBA. Her latest project is the design and illustration of a book for teaching phonics to preschoolers.

Kay Gorman moved to Colorado from Florida, where she was head designer and public relations/advertising manager for a chain of department stores. She is experienced in layout as well as in graphic techniques, and has contributed some of her ad expertise to our designs.

Mike Mancarella, one of the authors of this book, is responsible for the layouts suggested in "Very Simple Projects," as well as for a number of the graphics in the book. He is a graduate of the Colorado Institute of Art and has his own company, Communications, which specializes in commercial design of all kinds. He is also an accomplished photographer.

Rob Phillips also trained at the Colorado Institute of Art. A talented cartoonist and illustrator, he has illustrated a number of books for Libraries Unlimited. A freelance artist, he resides in Louisville, Colorado.

Tom Strang, whose specialty is technical art, gained his first experience at an ad agency in Detroit. After coming to Colorado, he worked for the development company Mission Viejo, and currently is working as a freelance artist. He lives in Littleton, Colorado.

South Park Graphics, a full-service commercial printing firm in Littleton, Colorado, provided many of the enlargements and reductions of art work used in this book and were very helpful in developing the tables of costs for printing. They are design consultants and a major supplier of printed goods for the Mission Viejo Company and Mile High United Way, Denver.

PART 1
Graphic Techniques

Clip Art & Libraries
What This Book Can Do for You

Today's libraries need to face the challenge of capturing public attention. They must present themselves in a way that will compete effectively with other advertising media by using promotional techniques that have proven successful in the commercial sector for years. The library's image often suffers from old-fashioned concepts; a good publicity program means better communication and a chance to do something about that image. Patrons should be informed about new developments and programs. This should be done in such a way that the public knows that the library cares about its patrons and that it provides quality services. One of the simplest ways to improve library communications is to create high-quality printed materials to convey your message. These materials might include newsletters, posters, notices, memos, handouts, bibliographies, bookmarks, signs, annual reports, and any other printed materials. These products can be much more effective if they are dressed up with clip art so that they look professional and are attractive to the eye.

Clip art includes any type of art or design that has already been created and can be cut out and used (with or without modifications) to enhance the written word. Clip art can be found in many places: commercial clip art books (such as this one), clip art services (generally expensive, but excellent), computer programs (such as Print Shop™), and in common sources such as magazines, posters, or junk mail. A word of caution, however: There are copyright guidelines to be considered whenever you use something created by someone else. Fair use implies that you can make an unspecified number of copies of art, provided that it is for in-house productions and is not to be resold in whole or in part. If you have questions or concerns about using material from another source, consult a trustworthy guide to copyright law.

Most of us are not blessed with extraordinary artistic talent, and even if we were, using clip art is frequently a faster way of obtaining the effect we want. By combining clip art with lettering, color, and text, the novice as well as the professional can produce a high-quality design and do it inexpensively. Clip art adds a dimension to in-house projects that is obtainable in no other way.

The purpose of part 1 of this book is to acquaint you with the steps to be taken to plan and create a high-quality printed product. It covers planning, the tools necessary for doing a **layout** (a diagram and instructions for typesetting and placement of illustrations), where to get lettering and how to use it, the use of different papers and color, and how to choose and deal with a printer. With a little practice, YOU, the librarian, will feel confident in designing with art and print, and you will be proud of the visual communications your efforts bring forth.

Planning for the Professional Look
Key Decisions

When you venture into a new printing or publicity project, planning is probably the most important step you will take and one that will make the difference between success and failure. Best results will be obtained if you proceed on a step-by-step basis. In planning your newsletter, bulletin board, poster, children's activity, etc., you need to consider all the steps listed below and ask yourself several questions.

Define the Purpose of the Project

Who is the audience? What is the theme or message? What benefits will your audience realize from your effort? What do you really hope to accomplish with your project?

Decide on the Format

Which design approach will have the most impact on this audience? (High school students may react better to a poster than a flyer; parents may prefer a flyer.) Different techniques and materials are required when making a poster for display or creating a newsletter that will be produced month after month. The **trim size** (finished size) of the project will certainly have to be considered. Cost may be a factor. Can you afford color if you are printing outside your institution? Will colored paper be effective? If you are mailing a flyer or announcement (or a catalog), postal regulations regarding size and weight will be a factor. Consult the Postal Service before getting too involved in any particular format. Consistency is important in any recurring project, such as a newsletter. You might want to design a **headline** (bold or **display type**, used to draw the reader's attention) for your newsletter and set up regular column features. How many copies will you have to print each month? Can you line up people to regularly contribute items to your newsletter?

How Much Copy Is Necessary?

Look at the amount of text required for your project and think about the illustrations needed. Will they fit in the allotted space? There should be lots of white space left on the finished piece to give the eye a rest. Generally, the best copy is the briefest. Don't insult the intelligence of your audience, but do use headlines and subheads (smaller headlines) liberally to aid the reader who wants to skim. Advertising experts agree that a benefit of some kind should be a prominent part of sales copy. For example, the library could be offering an opportunity for personal or cultural growth and enrichment, entertainment, or an educational experience. **RULE:** Keep it simple for best results.

Bringing Ideas Together

After the text has been written it should be compared with the illustrations that will accompany it to see if both will fit in the allotted space. Decide on the finished size of your piece and pencil in where you think the pictures, headlines, and body copy will look the best. Measure the **art** (all nontext material) you have selected to determine whether it needs to be reduced or enlarged (see page 34). If you don't have a photocopier that will reduce and enlarge, cut out pieces of paper the approximate size you want the finished art to be, make a copy of the text, and move them around on your sketch to see how they relate to each other. You'll probably change your mind a number of times, but this step is essential to assure the most attractive piece possible.

Printing, Binding, & Folding Requirements

The choice of reproduction and binding or folding depends on a number of factors: Will you have multiple sheets to attach together, how many copies are needed, can the project be done in-house (photocopied or on a mimeograph), what is your budget, and will colored ink be considered (can you afford it? do you need it?)? The way the piece will be printed and bound affects the way you prepare the art work.

A thorough evaluation of these factors will help you determine what method is best for you: doing it yourself, sending out for a quick-print job, or the use of a full-service printer. The more complicated the job, the longer it will take, and the more costly it will be. The choice is yours, and individual situations and requirements must be taken into account in your decision.

Examples of printing costs that will give you an idea of how much colored ink will cost compared to black ink only are given on page 42. Be sure to consult a number of local printers before making a solid commitment to your format, ink colors, etc.—the printer's costs may be prohibitive, or there may be alternative ways of producing the project that will save you money and be just as attractive. Professional printers can be of enormous assistance in the planning stage, so don't hesitate to call on them whenever a question arises about ink, paper, format, binding requirements, turn-around times, delivery, etc.

Clip It, Trim It, Glue It
Tools for the Designer

With a few basic tools, top quality brochures, flyers, newsletters, announcements, and posters can quickly be created. Within these pages are ideas to stimulate and inspire you. A totally new image can often be created by combining two or more illustrations with text, and by cutting, trimming, and pasting, a new look can emerge.

The various stages of a particular method to be used are explained with text and illustrations, and highlight the process and the end product expected. Proceed slowly at first and remember that effective communication with the target audience is the goal. Carefully developed projects should be simple and attractive and designed to keep people informed. A way to build on the process of communication is to take your creative thoughts and proceed through this idea book for inspiration.

To begin, you will need only the items discussed below. Assembling all the tools necessary before you begin will save time and frustration later. Average prices are indicated for most items as each is discussed.

Paper   Erasers
Illustration board   Pens and markers
Rulers   Correction fluid
T-squares   Masking tape
Triangles   Rubber cement and thinner
X-Acto™ knife and blades   Glue
Scissors   Burnisher
Pencils   Drawing board

Paper

Sketching Paper

There are two kinds of paper you will find very useful: tracing and layout. Tracing paper (9-by-12-inch pad, $3.00) is ideal for tracing details accurately but has a slightly grayish cast. Layout paper (9-by-12-inch pad, $5.00) is whiter and not quite as transparent, but still has enough transparency to enable you to trace easily. In pad form, most paper comes in standard sizes, ranging from about 9 by 12 inches to 19 by 24 inches.

Illustration Board

Generally available in two surfaces, smooth and **laid** finish, illustration board (15-by-20 inches, $5.00/pkg. of 4) is a heavy paper, brilliant white, with about 50 percent rag content. The smooth surface is suitable for all illustrations and hand lettering where detail is important. The laid finish, which is slightly pebbled, is more elegant and suitable for work such as invitations.

Rulers

An 18-inch etched steel ruler ($6.00) is essential for all kinds of measuring and determining sizes for art work and text. Be sure the ruler is graduated in inches (calibrated in sixteenths) on one edge, with a **pica** (approximately one-sixteenth of an inch; 6 picas equal approximately one inch) rule on the other edge (see page 12 for a discussion of picas). Steel rulers have sufficient weight so they won't slip under pressure and provide a sturdy guide for cutting with an **X-Acto knife** (a lightweight knife ideal for cutting around intricate art work).

T-Squares

A T-square ($9.00) has a crossbar attached perpendicular to one end of the long blade, much like a ruler. When you butt the crossbar flush against the side of a drawing board, vertical and horizontal lines can be drawn truly square. The T-square is also used to determine if art work and text are aligned properly. The head of the T-square should be solidly fixed to the ruler portion. For most projects the 24-inch size is best, but it is a good idea to select a size that accommodates the size of your drawing surface. The least expensive T-square is made of wood and is acceptable for most art work. However, if you are going to use it for a cutting edge, be sure to get a steel one.

Triangles

Triangles are used with a T-square to square up art work and text and to provide accurate 30 degree, 45 degree, or 60 degree angles, and can be used like a ruler for working with pencil, marker, or pen. A 12-inch triangle ($5.50) is the most versatile size. Do not use plastic triangles for cutting edges; once nicked, the plastic triangle is useless.

X-Acto Knife & Blades

X-Acto knives and blades are made of lightweight aluminum and are ideal for any art project. Blades come in many sizes and shapes and have plastic safety caps for blade tips. A number 11 or number 16 blade is very versatile and comes in a safety dispenser. A knife and blade combination will cost about $6.00. Blades are also available in bulk packed containers and cost about $17.00 per 100.

While scissors are ideal for cutting around objects, you will find that the X-Acto knife, designed to fit the hand, is sharper, more easily maneuverable in small spaces and around tight corners, such as trimming out clip art, and useful for cutting heavier materials also, such as thin cardboard used for posters.

Scissors

While any type of scissors will do, editor's shears (8-inch, $18.00) have long, slim, tapered blades, and are precision ground for smooth cutting. True accuracy is necessary when cutting typeset copy, art work, and other materials, and these fine scissors are ideal for general art work.

Pencils

Pencils are rated in degrees of hardness: "H" is hard, "B" is soft.

The most useful pencil for general use is probably either the 2H (medium hard) or 2B (medium soft). An HB is good for general sketching and layout. Softer pencils may smudge and need sharpening more frequently. Absolutely essential to any project that may be printed later is a **nonreproducing blue pencil** (see page 38). This pencil, used extensively in the commercial art field, does not photograph when printing plates are made.

Erasers

For general purposes the most popular eraser is the **art gum eraser**. It is nonabrasive and good for erasing pencil lines; it does, however, leave crumbs on the art work, so be very careful when brushing them away. The **kneaded eraser** ($6.00/dozen) is a pliable material, which cleans the drawing surface without leaving crumbs. Because it can stretch to fit your hand and be molded into shapes, it is useful for cleaning up corners or other delicate areas of art work. A **pick-up eraser** is used for picking up bits of dried rubber cement.

Pens & Markers

Felt-tip pens and markers come in a variety of colors and tip widths and are useful in highlighting or adding color to art projects. Markers dry almost instantly and are smudgeproof, and with the exception of black, the colors are transparent. Ball point pens can be used on general art work but they have a tendency to smear and feather around the edges; to avoid bleeding of the ink into unwanted areas, use a very fine quality paper or illustration board for projects that will require ink and marker work.

Correction Fluid

White-out or correction fluid ($1.50) is useful for touching up projects and erasing lines and shadows for projects that will later be printed or photocopied. It is applied sparingly with a light dot pattern, not brushed, and letters can be restruck over it with a typewriter or printed or drawn over with pens and markers.

Pentel™ sells a correction pen that is very convenient for small areas. The fluid is applied from a pinpoint applicator, and is suitable for use with typewriter, pen ink, and photocopying corrections.

Masking Tape

Masking tape (we recommend Scotch™ brand, ½-inch by 60 yds., $3.50/roll) comes in a variety of widths, but ½-inch or ¾-inch is the best size for most projects. White is preferable since it is less distracting on white paper projects. It makes photoreproduction less of a chore, since it helps to reduce the need to **opaque** (paint with white paint or correction fluid) shadows.

Rubber Cement & Thinner

One-coat rubber cement is an excellent adhesive for all kinds of wrinkle-free pasting. Apply the cement to one of the two surfaces to be pasted together. While the cement is wet it can be repositioned repeatedly. Purchase is most economical in the quart ($5.00) or gallon ($19.00) size. Pint-sized dispensers ($4.50) with a cap and brush depth adjustment are handy to use. Rubber cement will thicken, but by adding thinner ($3.00/pint) and shaking the bottle the solution will be restored to the proper consistency.

You may also find a rubber cement pick-up eraser helpful to remove excess cement after it has dried around the edges of your art. Rubbing will also remove the excess, but could result in displacing the art or smudging.

Rubber cement is potentially combustible when placed or stored near heat. There is a noncombustible type available for classroom use.

Glue

Glue sticks ($0.80) are useful for cardboard, fabric, photographs, drawings, etc. A screw-on top keeps the contents fresh. Elmer's Glue-All™ (8 oz., $2.00) bonds all porous materials together. It dries transparent, and won't stain. Plastic squeeze bottles with applicator tips are available in sizes up to one quart.

Burnisher

A **burnisher** is used to assure adherence of rub-on typefaces (see page 18) and to crease folds in paper. They can be made of many substances, including plastic, animal bone, or metal. Some have a "ball" end for individual letters of press-on type and a "bone" end for burnishing large areas. A burnisher costs about $3.50.

Drawing Board

Any sturdy table could be used as a work surface, but an artist's drawing board ($25.00) is well worth considering if you can afford it. Drawing boards have adjustable legs, and a nonglare white working surface, and are portable. They are available in sizes from 18 by 24 inches to 24 by 36 inches, and larger. The board must have a true-edge, a metal strip already attached to the lefthand side, which is used for lining up your T-square and allows it to slide up and down easily.

A luxury item, but nevertheless extremely useful if you can afford it, is an illuminated tracing board ($125.00). The illumination comes from below and shines through a frosted glass top to reduce eye strain. The table has a true-edge and can be propped up at the back end to tilt at an angle, which facilitates use and helps to eliminate back strain, since it can be adjusted for personal preference. It is light in weight and can sit flat on any work surface. With illumination from below you can position or trace materials with ease, and the table also serves as a compact, all-purpose work surface. If you simply cannot afford an illuminated board, don't forget that for positioning or tracing purposes, a window will do in a pinch!

The ABCs of Type
Laying the Foundation

Typefaces come in all styles, both simple and ornate. There are two basic kinds: **serif** and **sans serif**. Serif typefaces are a little more formal and also easier to read if the type is small.

RULE: Don't mix too many typefaces, particularly of the same kind. In general, use a serif face with a sans serif face for the best effect (e.g., headlines in serif and the text copy in sans serif, or vice versa).

All letters and punctuation align on an imaginary horizontal reference line called a **baseline**.

When you are preparing art work of any kind you will want to use a baseline, either drawn with very light pencil lines or nonreproducing blue pencil, to be sure everything is straight.

Width & Height Variations

Variety in typefaces is achieved by varying the width and height of the letters.

Medium: a letter weight often used for text because of its readability.

This is medium.

Bold: printing made to appear darker, thicker, and more pronounced than medium letters.

This is bold.

Italic: letters that slant to the right and have rounded lines.

This is italic.

Condensed: a squeezed up version of regular type that takes less space in a line than the same letters would in standard size.

These are word spaces.	Normal
These are word spaces.	Condensed

Extended: a wider version. Also called *expanded type*.

These are word spaces.	Normal
These are word spaces.	Expanded

Serif & Sans Serif Type

A serif is the flat stroke that projects from the top and bottom of the main stroke of a letter. Some printed letters have no serifs at all; these letters are called sans serif.

ABCDEFG ◄ serif

Serif letters

ABCDEFG

Sans serif letters

The addition of the serif not only adds decoration to the letter, but also aids the eye of the reader in passing from one letter to another.

Points & Picas

The two basic units used in **typography** (the art of combining different heights and weights of letters to produce pleasing results) are called **points** and **picas**. The smaller unit is the point. There are 12 points in one pica. There are 6 picas in one inch. Study the figure below. These measurements are fundamental to printed type and you will encounter them frequently in literature dealing with typesetting and graphic art. Pica and point scales and rulers are available in plastic and are essential if you are working with typeset copy.

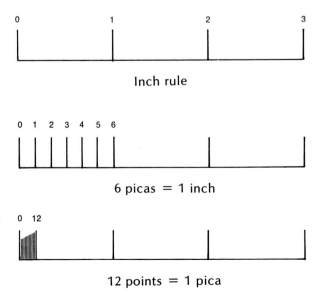

Inch rule

6 picas = 1 inch

12 points = 1 pica

Picture This
Designing with Type

If you won't be limited to a typewriter, think about the typeface that appeals to you. A typeset piece looks extremely professional, far more so than something produced on a typewriter.

Call several printers who advertise typesetting services and find out costs. These printers will also have catalogs of different typefaces available for inspection. You should be able to order headlines, subheads, or text copy in a variety of styles and sizes. Try to pick typefaces that will be appropriate to the content of your material. Will it be easy to read for the chosen audience? Will it be read by children or adults? The size and style of the typeface are influenced by both the message and the audience.

Consider legibility. You are communicating a message in the clearest way possible. The type will be more or less legible, depending not only on its size and style, but also on the way it is arranged on the page. Type should be comfortable to read. If you have much information to display on a page don't try to force everything into a small area: be selective and creative, and eliminate and condense to get your message across. Use italics with care. They are used mainly for emphasis and generally are not to be read in sentence form. The same goes for ornate type of any kind: use it sparingly.

There are no hard and fast rules for proper **word spacing** (the space between words), because so much depends on the style of typeface chosen. However, condensed faces usually need less word spacing and extended faces more.

Leading

Leading is the insertion of small additional spaces between lines of type for easier reading. Although readability is improved with a little additional leading, lines may appear to drift apart with too much leading, and the type will appear grayer and smaller.

In our twenty-third year, our aim at Libraries Unlimited is still to publish both responsibly and responsively in view of the changing needs and interests of the professional community whom we serve.

In our twenty-third year, our aim at Libraries Unlimited is still to publish both responsibly and responsively in view of the changing needs and interests of the professional community whom we serve.

In our twenty-third year, our aim at Libraries Unlimited is still to publish both responsibly and responsively in view of the changing needs and interests of the professional community whom we serve.

The choice of typeface, type size, word spacing, and length of line will all affect the amount of leading needed. It is your goal to make the project as attractive as possible, and leading is one consideration that cannot be overlooked.

Justified Margins

When all the lines of type are the same length, the type is **justified**. Justified type is recommended whenever there is a lot of material to be read. There is some risk that poor word spacing will result because of the justification, so be careful to plan the piece accordingly.

> In our twenty-third year, our aim at Libraries Unlimited is still to
> publish both responsibly and responsively in view of the changing
> needs and interests of the professional community whom we serve.

Unjustified Margins

Unjustified margins are when the lines are aligned all right or all left on the page, with the margin ragged. Interesting arrangements can be created using this method, but it is best suited to short copy.

> In our twenty-third year, our aim at Libraries Unlimited is
> still to publish both responsibly and responsively in view
> of the changing needs and interests of the professional community

Centered Copy

Centered lines (one over the other) creates visual interest and ensures even word spacing. Try to avoid using lines of the same or similar lengths when centering, to keep the eye moving from left to right. Centering all the copy is most suitable for small amounts of copy.

> In our twenty-third year,
> our aim at Libraries Unlimited is still to publish
> both responsibly and responsively in view of the changing needs

Asymmetrical Placement

With **asymmetrical** placement no predictable pattern develops in the length or placement of lines. This method can be very dramatic on posters, advertisements, and other displays that are used to attract attention. There are no rules to follow: place the lines as they look best. Leading should be generous to prevent fatigue and help the reader locate the next line easily. If this method of arrangement is handled carelessly it can be a disaster and result in material that is difficult to read and distracting for the reader.

> In our twenty-third year,
> our aim at
> Libraries Unlimited
> is still to publish both responsibly and responsively
> in view of the changing needs and interests of

Quick & Dirty
Instant Lettering

Working with **instant lettering** (letters, numbers, and punctuation that are cut from acetate backing or rubbed-off onto art work) sheets is one way to produce creative, unique art projects. With the most limited skill you can produce remarkable results. The initial investment is modest. Most sheets cost $3.50 to $9.00 each. These sheets include numbers, full alphabets, punctuation, and other symbols in a particular typeface and size. Borders and other design elements are available, as are foreign alphabets such as Greek, Cyrillic, Arabic, and Hebrew. Special interest sheets are also available for music, chemical equations, etc., and customized sheets can be designed to eliminate the need to recreate or reproduce repetitive items used frequently, such as logos, special school and library symbols, etc.

The two most popular types of lettering sheets are rub-on and cut-out. Rub-on type is applied directly to the face of the art work using a burnisher; cut-out is cut from the clear acetate sheet with an X-Acto knife and applied to the face of the art.

Instant lettering catalogs are available free from art supply stores. They include examples of all typefaces available, border designs, symbols, arrows, stars, decorative dots, and shading and textures.

Materials Required

Burnisher	T-square
Hard lead pencil (use on posters or display art)	Triangles
Nonreproducing blue pencil	X-Acto knife and blades

Cut-Out Type

Cut-out type is appropriate for any project that will later be printed. The type is crackproof, scratch resistant, and heat resistant, and can be repositioned during initial application to the art. Cut-out type is best for items to be printed later because it has a clear acetate backing around the letters that will show if used for posters or other display materials.

Professional looking art work requires straight, even lines. After deciding on the layout, tape the illustration board or paper to your work surface for stability. Mark guidelines on the board or paper with a nonreproducing blue pencil.

Cut lightly around the letter with the X-Acto knife. Turn the knife blade so it is parallel to the sheet and slide the blade under the letter and lift off the backing sheet.

Position the letter on the art work by aligning with the guideline. Lay the letter into place and smooth with your finger. Overlaps should be avoided by trimming very close to the letter, then lightly burnishing the letters until the edges disappear after you place the letters on the art. If letters are not burnished properly, shadows may occur around the edges on the finished copy and may require opaquing or touch-up.

Shading & Background Textures

Special effects can be created using shading and background textures that are available on cut-out sheets. To apply the shading/background texture to the art, cut and remove enough shading to cover the designated area plus a small border. Place the cut-out piece directly on the art work. Using an X-Acto knife, cut lightly through the shading on the outline of the area to be shaded/textured. Remove excess shading by lifting with the knife edge and pulling gently. Burnish the shaded/textured area to ensure adherence. (See page 25 for a discussion of photographic screens.)

The examples below are from the *Formatt Cut-Out Acetate Graphic Art Aids* catalog.

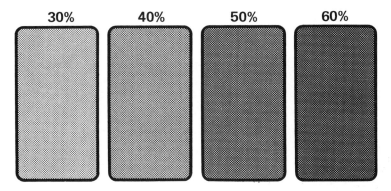

Various degrees of shading (screens) available on cut-out sheets.

Background textures: the possibilities are limitless for creating unique effects using these sheets.

Rub-On Type

Rub-on typeface and symbol sheets are appropriate for use on any piece of art work, whether for posters and display items or for material that will be printed later. Rub-on sheets are more delicate than cut-out sheets, so handle them with care. Cracking and flaking can occur if the surface on which they are applied should bend or crease, so be especially careful when removing the piece from the work surface. Special storage is required to ensure long life and durability (see page 20).

In order to avoid having your guidelines show along the baseline of your letters, prepare the guidelines on a separate piece of paper which can be laid underneath the project you are applying the letters to. An illuminated drawing table is ideal for use with rub-on letters. If you don't have such a table, you can generally see the faint guidelines through heavy paper or you could use a window, although positioning the letters and rubbing them on would be uncomfortable.

If you are working on illustration board (such as for a poster), draw your guidelines with your X-Acto knife. Do not press too heavily into the board because you don't want to score the surface deeply; your line will be clearly visible as you apply the letter, but will appear to disappear when the letters are all in place. It is best to mark your guidelines the approximate length of the words you will be applying, so you don't have an obvious grooved line between individual words.

Work from the top of the letter to the bottom. The letter will appear to "gray out" as it transfers. Gently peel the sheet back from the top. Keep it firmly in place with your hand while you check to be sure the entire letter transferred. If the letter hasn't transferred completely, place the sheet back into position and rub the entire letter again. Once the letter is transferred, cover with the backing (or a piece of clean paper if there is no backing sheet) and rub over it with the burnisher to ensure adhesion. Slight breaks in the letters can be touched up with a black felt tip pen.

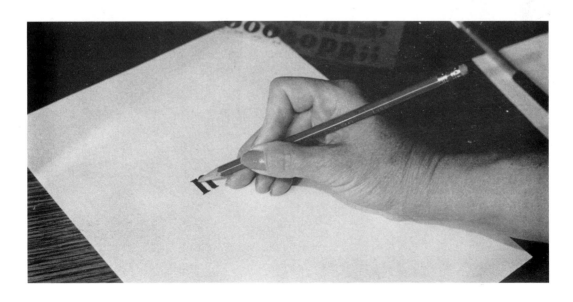

Correcting Mistakes

To correct problems such as broken letters, misspelled words, etc., take a piece of masking tape or any low-tack tape and place it on top of the letter. It will lift off the surface of the art work. If the material is already burnished and the letter will not lift, moisten a cotton swab with rubber cement thinner and wipe it off. Dry the area completely before applying another letter. Rub-on type takes some getting used to, so practice first on something unimportant.

Storage of Sheets

Flat storage is recommended. Flat file folders work well and are inexpensive. Rub-on sheets are delicate. Flaking of letters can occur, so handle them with extreme care. If your project has a long-term use or will be handled extensively, or you wish to place it in an archive, it is recommended that you have a **photomechanical transfer (PMT)** (an inexpensive copy of the art work that retains the detail of the original; see page 36 for discussion and costs) made of the art, or that you use cut-out acetate letters, which are more permanent than rub-on, instead. Any commercial printer can supply PMTs.

Border Boards

Border boards are pieces of light cardboard with decorative borders printed in black ink. Overall sizes available are 7½ by 10 inches, 8½ by 11 inches, and 10 by 13½ inches, and they can be purchased from most art supply stores. They have designated space to add unique messages. Vertical and horizontal guidelines are marked in nonreproducing blue. Since the board itself provides most of the decoration you need, the boards can be used to produce distinctive advertisements, mailing pieces, and invitations with little effort. Border boards are not suitable for display since the blue guidelines show under the copy placed on them. They are used for projects that will be printed later, either commercially or with a photocopier.

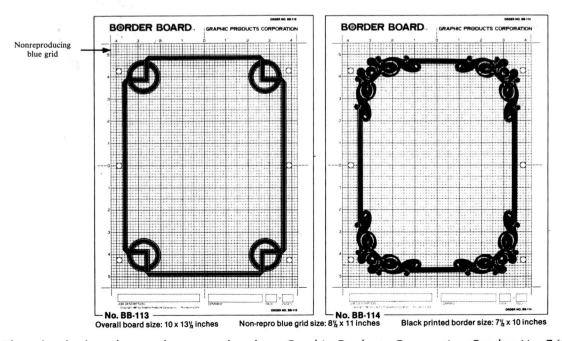

No. BB-113
Overall board size: 10 x 13½ inches   Non-repro blue grid size: 8½ x 11 inches   Black printed border size: 7½ x 10 inches

These border board examples were taken from Graphic Products Corporation *Catalog No. 7* (1981).

Border Tapes

Decorative border tapes are available in a convenient "tape pen" (a plastic cylinder shaped to fit the hand that dispenses a tape line), and come in many colors, patterns, and point sizes. To use the tape pen, draw a guideline (use either very light lead pencil line or nonreproducing blue pencil) and attach the tape end to the surface. Draw the tape along the guideline with a steady pull. Press down gently so the tape stays in place. Burnish lightly. Tapes can be repositioned by placing the tip of an X-Acto knife underneath and lifting. If any tape adheres to the art work, scrape it away with the knife tip, or use a small piece of adhesive tape to pull it off.

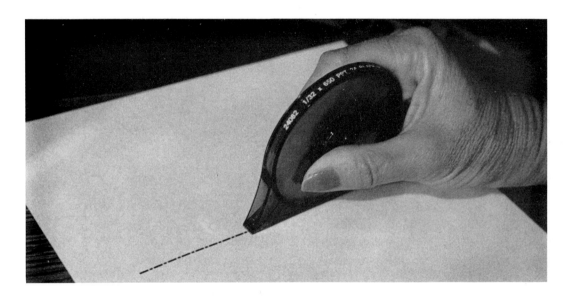

Lettering Stencils & Templates

Frequently the words **stencil** (material such as paper or cardboard perforated with letters or designs whose outlines are traced onto a surface) and **template** (much like a stencil, but has risers to keep it off the work surface and avoid smearing when using ink pens to trace the letters) are used interchangeably, but there are differences between them and the uses for which they are ideally designed. Both templates and stencils come in several formats, including cardboard, wood, metal, and paper. Both contain full alphabets, numbers, and punctuation marks.

Cardboard stencils are very inexpensive and can be used for lettering with pen or with spray paints. They can be discarded after each use and replaced often. Metal templates are used most frequently with pencils and pens. Most templates have risers which make them ideal for use with ink pens. The built-in risers separate the template slightly from the drawing surface, which helps to eliminate smearing while you are using it. If the template you are using does not have a riser you can make one by taping a penny on the underside. Risers also make it easy to pick up and reposition the template without your fingers scratching or smearing the surface of the project.

Vinyl Sign Letters

Versatile vinyl die-cut letters, numbers, and symbols are available at most stationery and art supply stores. These self-adhesive sign letters stay fresh and clean looking, wash clean with water, and adhere to most surfaces inside and out. The letters have crisp edges, which improves legibility of signs. You can create signs for exhibitions, direction boards, displays, posters, or equipment identification labels for your library or school without a big investment. The letters come in various sizes and colors, and some international symbols are available.

Shaky Hand Syndrome
Freehand Lettering

Freehand lettering can be pleasing to the eye, attention getting, and unique. Letterheads, posters, and notices can all benefit from this informal lettering technique.

Materials Required

The tools and materials you will need for learning to freehand letter consist of a drawing board, paper, pencils, pens, black ink, an art gum or kneaded rubber eraser, a T-square, a triangle, and white watercolor paint for removing unwanted edges on your letters.

Paper used for finished work should have a hard surface suitable for pen and ink renderings. A very smooth surfaced paper is easier to work with than one with any pebbling, or "tooth."

For drawing or sketching in letters use a B or HB pencil. An electric pencil sharpener is helpful for maintaining a sharp point.

A square-cut steel pen ($13.00) will be necessary for drawing the practice strokes and letters. These pens come in a variety of sizes, each size making a different thickness of line. Pens require some care. They should be cleaned thoroughly after each use, since ink left in the pen will harden and spread the nib, making the pen useless.

Technique

A few suggestions to get you started will result in better first efforts. *Get comfortable.* Don't grip your pencil tightly or use so much pressure that you make hard work of drawing basic strokes. Try for a free and easy touch. Aim for well-proportioned letters and good spacing. Measuring with a ruler and placing letters equal distances apart will not achieve the spontaneity that makes freehand lettering so attractive. From time to time look at your letters *upside down.* This provides a check on their straightness and uniformity of curves. Use a ruler only for the guidelines within which letters will be placed. Remember, spontaneity is essential in freehand lettering.

Sketch letters in pencil first. Check the spacing. Top and bottom guidelines are then drawn to the proper height of the letters. Pencil in any special details of the letters before finishing them in ink.

The ends of the strokes for many styles of letters may be finished with a serif. The appearance of the letter will be changed significantly by the addition of serifs. Varying the thickness of the stroke will also change the character of the letters.

Felt-tip markers are ideal for practice lettering. Use the narrow edge for outlines and the wider edge for filling in and squaring or rounding off the curves of the letters. When using felt-tip markers do not repeat the stroke; this results in different densities of the ink on the paper because of the different hand pressure.

The word "calligraphy" implies beautiful or elegant handwriting. A pen with a nib tip (fine, medium, broad) is used to produce the letters. Calligraphy is ideal for diplomas and certificates, poetry, etc. Inexpensive sets ($12.00) include a pen with nib tips, ink cartridges in various colors for decorative work, and an instruction book.

Forming Letters

Sharpen a flat, soft sketching pencil to a chiseled edge. If the lead is the right width, only one stroke of the pencil will make the vertical part of the letter.

Add serifs with pointed pencil. Angle pencil for outer and inner curves of the letters.

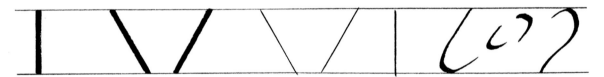

Basic strokes in drawing vertical letters.

Let Me Count the Ways
Layouts

A layout (or dummy) is a plan of what you hope the finished project will look like. It provides a general picture of the finished piece with all the text and art in place. A complete layout includes:

- text copy to be included
- style of typefaces
- position of type in relation to illustrations
- kind and color of paper
- overall size of project
- color of ink to be used
- fold, if appropriate (see pages 27-28)

Professional results are rarely achieved on the first try. Some designers spend hours preparing many **rough sketches**, then discard them all to begin over again with a fresh idea. Each sketch should build on the previous one, eliminating the weak areas as a new sketch is created. Put your ideas on paper rapidly. Experiment with many different layouts, vary the dimensions of the overall piece, try a few colors to see how it looks. Make a preliminary layout of the entire project and the lettering to be used (either freehand or instant press type). Sketch in any pictures, drawings, or other elements to see how they will relate to each other.

Use areas of white space to make the design elements more prominent. White space is actually a background for the art work and type, so use it effectively. Emphasis can be added to headlines by surrounding them with white space, and it makes the headlines easier to read also.

Think about using boxes to draw attention to elements that might otherwise be overlooked. A portion of the art work can be boxed, photographs and illustrations can be highlighted with a box, material can be **reversed** (white letters on a dark background) in a box, and **screens** (fine dot pattern that results in various intensities of original color; see pages 17 and 41 for a discussion and costs) can be used to lead the eye to important information. Everything should be in harmony and good taste, and only through experimentation with the various elements can the desired results be achieved.

Arranging Type & Illustrations

Provide a focal point for the reader. Avoid clutter and confusion, and think simple. If you have two pages that will be facing each other, concentrate your creative efforts on both pages at the same time to avoid creating pages that lack harmony when placed side by side. Numerous examples of pleasing page arrangements, both for text only and text with illustrations, are provided below.

Page arrangements for text only.

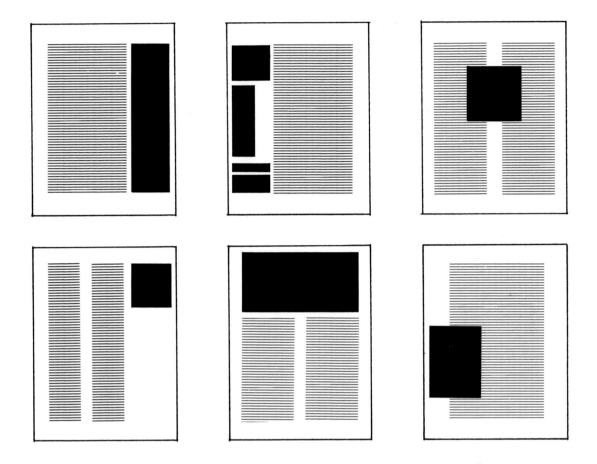

Page arrangements for text and illustrations.

Various Ways of Folding a Sheet

The way in which you fold your flyer, newsletter, or bulletin also says something about it. Folds can be formal or whimsical (as can the size and shape of the piece). To experiment, tape several pieces of paper together until you have a piece that is the size you think you will need. Sometimes you need to experiment with several sizes and folds. For example, if you are doing a brochure to let your patrons know about new books and activities, you might have a lot to say, more than will fit on an 8½-by-11-inch sheet. Try taping two together, then folding them in half and in half again. Several convenient sized pieces can be obtained using an 11-by-17-inch sheet, which is also a very common size and therefore economical. A brochure could also be folded in thirds, but horizontally. The diagrams on page 28 illustrate these folding techniques.

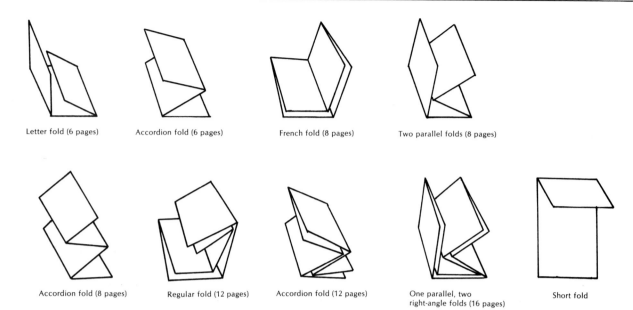

Letter fold (6 pages)   Accordion fold (6 pages)   French fold (8 pages)   Two parallel folds (8 pages)

Accordion fold (8 pages)   Regular fold (12 pages)   Accordion fold (12 pages)   One parallel, two right-angle folds (16 pages)   Short fold

Some papers don't fold well because of the surface texture used on them, so if you have any questions about what paper is best suited to certain kinds of folds, consult a professional printer.

Over the Rainbow
Using Color Effectively

Color adds excitement and personality to art work. It costs more to commercially print a piece with color because of the technology, extra steps, and printing techniques involved, so color must be used with care in order to get the biggest effect from the smallest investment. When color is used correctly it can clarify the message, improve communication, and enrich the project:

- Use color as background

- Use color as a decorative tool

- Use color to emphasize specific elements

- Use color to separate one set of items from another

It is very important to remember that ink is transparent. The color of the paper stock chosen can affect the color of the ink chosen. Colored paper stock tends to pull down the intensity of the ink applied to it, so when planning a project "think ink" before you get too far into your specifications. Lighter or pastel papers combine well with stronger ink colors. Combinations of ink and paper of the same color will be illegible. Consult your professional printer before you make a final selection. For a discussion of colored paper, see page 33.

Four-Color Process & Two-Color Printing

Four-Color Process

The technique used to print pictures in full, natural colors is called **four-color process**. There are four colors involved: yellow, red, blue, and black. Each of these colors is made on a separate printing plate; when they are superimposed one on top of the other a reproduction of natural colors results. Four-color printing is very expensive. Get estimates from local printers before making a commitment to the four-color process.

Two-Color Printing

Using two colors of ink (e.g., black and another color, or two colors, one of which is dark enough to use for text copy) is a very popular way to add pizzazz and sparkle for a small increase in cost. Choosing colors is confusing; the system for identifying color that is the most widely used is the Pantone Matching System.™ Books of ink samples (PMS books) are available from most art stores for about $15.00. Each color is assigned a code number and is reproduced on both shiny and dull paper. The number refers to an ink formula, and one can spend hours contemplating the possibilities of which color will go best with what. Don't try this if you are color blind!

Two-color work is less expensive to produce than four-color process because the presses needed to run the work are less expensive. Ink sample swatch books that have an acetate overlay with black and white type printed on it are available to help you visualize colors, and you can get an idea of what the color looks like in order to check readability. Use enough color to make the piece noticeable and worth the extra effort and expense. See page 42 for a comparison of printing in black ink only versus using colored ink, and on various sizes of paper. Projects that will be printed on two sides are also discussed.

From the Ground Up
Paper

Once you have your design and layout, you need to choose your paper. Paper comes in all kinds of weights, textures, and colors, with varying degrees of shininess, foldability, and durability.

Standard Sizes

The economics of printing and the cost of paper dictate the use of certain standardized sizes when possible. Paper sizes vary according to the grade of paper. Bond paper, used for letters and business forms, comes in a standard printing sheet of 17 by 22 inches. Offset paper and coated (shiny) stock come in 25 by 38 inches. Text paper, used for booklets and brochures, comes in 25 by 38 inches; cover stock, a much heavier weight than bond paper, measures 20 by 26 inches in standard size.

Weight

Paper weight ("basis weight") is measured in pounds per 500 sheets (a ream). Thus, a 20-pound bond paper in standard size printer's stock, 17 by 22 inches, would weigh 20 pounds. One ream of 8½-by-11-inch paper (one-fourth of a printer's standard sized sheet) would weigh 5 pounds. Papers are available from 20-pound to 175-pound and higher.

The weight of the stock chosen may be important if the piece will be mailed. It is wise to ask the paper supplier or printer to prepare a paper package that has the exact number of pages of your project so that it can be weighed before proceeding too far with the project. Lighter paper stock may save on postage and does not necessarily make the piece feel cheap or look flimsy.

Remember that the heavier the paper stock chosen, the more expensive it will be to produce. The additional cost can be justified by considering the look and feel of the finished product, and the fact that some projects prepared for mailing must meet certain postal regulations. Check with your local post office to see if your plans meet these regulations before you make a final decision on paper stock.

Opacity

An aspect of paper stock that helps prevent type from showing through from one side to the other is called **opacity**. If the printing on one side of the paper shows through to the other side of the paper, it is called **show-through**. The thicker the paper the less show-through. Request printed samples of paper stock so that you can make an intelligent decision about the weight of paper to be used. The less the paper costs, the greater the likelihood of show-through.

Coated (Shiny) Stock

Shininess is achieved by coating the paper with chemicals that close up the surface irregularities. Photographs will reproduce better on coated paper, screened illustrations will have better definition, and ink appears to have more depth.

Kinds of Paper

Each grade of paper serves a particular use. The most common classifications likely to be encountered for simple projects are bond, coated stock, text, cover, and offset. Some kinds of papers are more expensive than others, even though they weigh the same. Cost differences are due to surface textures and overall quality.

Bond. Used for letters and business forms. The surface is ideal for typewriter use and it accepts ink well for all business purposes. Most letterheads and business forms are 8½ by 11 inches.

Coated. This is a standard paper sheet to which a shiny surface has been added. Because of its smoothness and receptivity for ink, coated paper is used when high-quality printing is desired. Quick setting inks are used to maintain brilliant color and good gloss. Coated glossy stock comes in white and cream only.

Text. Text sheets come in many textures and attractive colors and are useful for announcements, booklets, brochures, and invitations. They accept colored inks well and are very popular for all printed projects.

Offset. Similar to coated and uncoated papers, offset paper is used extensively for all printed pieces. It is a little more expensive than text; it accepts ink very well and is easier for the printer to use when printing large blocks of solid color.

Cover. Heavier weight and matching colors are the main features of cover stock used mainly for booklets or office forms that require some rigidity. Special textures are available in a wide range of colors.

Texture

The texture of the paper stock chosen is important. **Woven** paper has a uniform, smooth surface. Laid paper has fine lines running through it, which are only truly visible when it is held up to the light. Offset papers are coated with sizing to make the surface less porous, which allows the ink to sit on the surface and not seep into the fibers. Each type of paper stock has unique qualities that make it suitable for different projects.

Finish

"Finish" is a term related to the smoothness of the paper. Antique, eggshell, and vellum are the customary finishes of uncoated paper. These papers can be coated to further improve the finish and smoothness.

Embossed patterns can be added to paper also, resulting in surface finishes such as linen, tweed, and pebble. These surface treatments are quite subtle, but do lend distinction to many paper sheets.

Colored

An unlimited range of color sheets is available from various paper supply houses or your printer. Because ink is transparent, there are some problems with colored stock. Printing photographs on colored stock can make them appear muddy and lifeless. If the colors of the paper and ink don't complement each other, the project will be unattractive and can even cause reader fatigue. On promotion pieces, the use of unique color combinations can be very exciting, but the result depends on subtle use of various colors of ink. Ask for a test run before committing to the entire project if in doubt.

If there is a need for repeated use of the same colored paper stock, be sure it will be available in the future. The color chosen could become a means of identification, just like a logo, so be sure adequate stock is available for long-range projects. Ordinary colors are generally well stocked, so it might be a good idea to consider these before selecting something special and unique.

A final note: Paper companies have wonderful packets which they give out to customers, usually those customers who are large users of paper. However, many are happy to have a customer (even a small customer) who is interested in their product, and they will give out some very interesting samples. ASK!

The Big & the Little of It
Reducing & Enlarging Illustrations

Several sizes of many of the illustrations in this book have been included for your convenience. However, if you need something enlarged or reduced, it is an easy matter to have it done photographically.

When you **scale** (determine the final dimensions of copy which is to be enlarged or reduced) art or text, it is difficult to predict whether it will become illegible when made smaller, or become fuzzy and distorted when enlarged. Two methods for finding out in advance what can be expected are outlined below.

1. Look at it through a reducing or magnifying glass. This will give a rough idea of what it will look like. An optical quality magnifying or reducing lens will cost about $15.00.

2. Have a **photostatic copy**, called a "stat" for short, made (see also PMTs, page 36). One 8½-by-11-inch shot will cost about $4.50. Prices vary according to the size required. If you have several originals that are to be reduced or enlarged to the same size, you may save money if you **gang run** them (running them at the same time).

If you are concerned primarily about the size of the illustration or text when enlarged or reduced, you can use a photocopier with a reducing/enlarging option. Many photocopiers allow you to choose the exact percent of reduction or enlargement in 1 percent increments. If the reduction isn't right to begin with, make a reduction of a reduction and vice versa. Most details will be lost in this process, but you can achieve something close to the actual size desired by using this method.

Proportion Wheel

A **proportion wheel** is the most widely used device for determining enlargement and reduction sizes, because it is compact and inexpensive. The larger the diameter readings given on the face of the wheel, the easier it is to read the various scales which mark off the percent desired. Wheels are available for $2.00-$6.00.

The proportion wheel is a very handy tool, consisting of two sliding circles, one smaller than the other. On each circle are marks representing inches. The inner one represents the original size of the piece of art (or headline, or photograph); the outer one, the desired future size. For example, you have a picture of a baby giraffe reading his book, but it measures 5¾ inches from the tip of his tail to the bottom of his book. You want it no larger than 3 inches. Line up 3 on the outside of the wheel, with 5¾ on the inside. The number in the window is 52 percent. You ask your printer to reduce the image to 52 percent when he prints.

This proportional scale can save you a lot of grief and guesswork when you are trying to scale and position art work, so be sure to have it handy at all times when you are planning your projects.

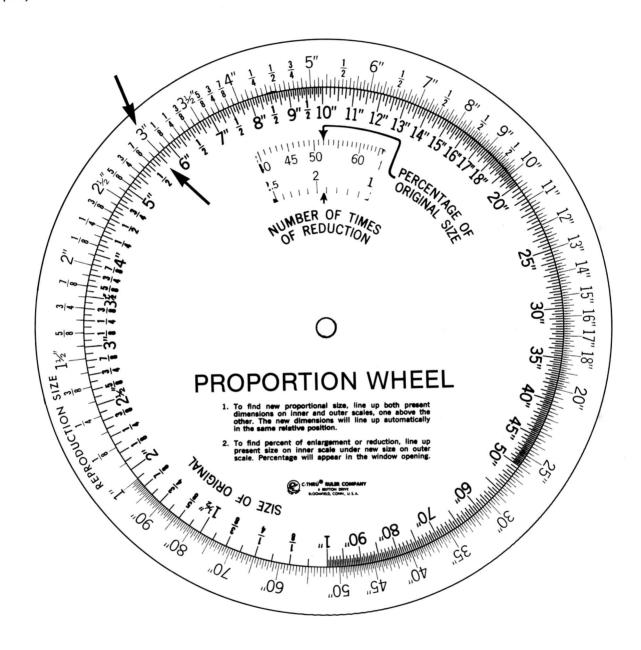

A Picture Is Worth a Thousand Words
Photographs

A photograph is actually made up of a number of tones ranging from white to black. The tones from one part of the photograph to another cannot be reproduced by printing directly from a photograph. By rephotographing the original photograph through a screen (see pages 17, 25, and 41), the tones are broken into a dot pattern. When the dots are tiny the image will be light gray; when there are no dots it appears white. Where the dots touch each other, the image is black. This is called a **halftone**. The finer the screen used, the closer the image will be to the original. A printer can advise what screen should be used for the desired effect.

Cropping a Photograph

If you do not want all parts of the photograph to print, you can **crop** it. To determine what your photograph will look like when cropped, cut two L-shaped pieces of paper or cardboard and lay them facing each other on the photograph. Overlap them slightly to create a border around the image area that you want. The image in the framed area is indicated to the printer by placing a flap of plain paper over the face of the photograph and drawing with pencil lines the part to be cut off. This will not affect the original photograph and tells the printer the exact part of the image you desire.

PMTs (Photomechanical Transfers)

A PMT is one of the most often used aids in commercial art. A PMT is a picture of existing art with far greater definition and detail than a photocopy can provide, and it is on slick paper so that it is **camera-ready** (all text and art in place and ready to be printed). Artists frequently request PMTs from their printer because they are inexpensive ($6.00 for a 9-by-12-inch shot and less for a smaller one), and because they can be shot at the exact proportion needed for the finished piece. They do lose some of the very fine detail of original art (if it has any), but can be vital for creating a realistic dummy. Both the PMT and original should accompany the piece to the printer.

A PMT can be made of line art or of type; a photograph must be made into a halftone. If you need a smaller or larger copy of any clip art in this book, request a PMT.

For some special effects that can be created by changing the dot pattern of an original photograph, see pages 167-71. A printer can determine the correct method to be used to reproduce the effects shown.

Line Art

Illustrations that are black and white, with no middle tones (grays), requiring halftone screens to reproduce well, are called **line art**. The clip art in this book is line art. Line art works well because it has no hard outline, as photographs do, and it can lend openness and informality to the project. Simple line drawings can be altered using various photomechanical variations also, and consultation with a printer can help determine what the final results of manipulating a drawing may be.

What Do You Mean, It's Not Straight?
Preparing Mechanicals

A **mechanical** is the complete original art and text ready for printing, with all the elements in position. The result is referred to as camera-ready copy.

Gathering the Pieces & Marking Them Up

Gather together all the tools and materials needed, along with the pieces of the project, such as text and art work selected. With scissors or an X-Acto knife, trim off all excess margins. Select paper or illustration board and secure it to the work surface with masking tape. Lightly mark guidelines to indicate the overall size of the project. If making a poster or other art work for display, use a hard lead pencil (guidelines will be erased later). If making a piece for printing, use nonreproducing blue pencil to draw the dimensions of the finished pieces, using the T-square for horizontal and vertical lines.

Folds are indicated with a lightly drawn broken line. To show where an illustration is to go on a page, draw a line (called a **keyline**) around the area using blue pencil, showing the dimensions of the graphic. Keylines can also be drawn in ink to be printed later (e.g., boxed copy). Identify in the block the name or number of the graphic to be placed there.

Pencils and ball point pen can smear, so be very selective about their use. Do not use transparent tape (Scotch tape) on mechanicals since it could appear as a shadow on the printed piece. Precise measurements and attention to detail are essential when preparing mechanicals. Smudges, dirt, excess glue, and poor alignment are very obvious on printed and folded pieces, so be precise when working on the art board. Use white correction fluid or white paint to correct minor mistakes and spots.

Assembling the Mechanical

Before you **paste up** all the design elements in their proper positions, take some time to proofread once more. Check for spelling mistakes and typographical errors. Make sure that nothing important has been left out. Ask a coworker to review the art work; it is easy to overlook your own mistakes. Check the graphics: make sure lines are drawn in properly, that the bottoms of columns line up, and, if the piece is multipaged, if there is a guide to tell readers where the material continues. Careful checking can mean the difference between a high-quality production and a disaster.

Apply a thin coat of rubber cement and place the elements on the illustration board (or paper) within the designated areas. Rubber cement remains workable for some time, so before pressing the pieces into place, be sure they are straight and aligned properly with other copy.

Printers prefer the use of rubber cement over tape of any kind to affix art work and text. Tape will photograph as a shadow on negatives and has to be opaqued out. Rubber cement, used sparingly, provides a permanent bond for the various pieces of the project.

Recording Instructions & Information

Indicate which areas are to be which color, drawing lines in nonreproducible blue pencil to each area from the margins. "Print all text black" is a frequent instruction. When indicating color, use the PMS number and the percent of that color you wish to print, for example, "100% PMS 186" is bright red; "30% PMS 186" will print as pink. (See the discussion of screens on pages 17, 25, and 41.)

Protect every piece of art work against damage by putting a flap over the face of it. Generally this will be tracing paper on which instructions to the printer are written. Don't write on the flap with ball point or felt tip pen because it might soak through and ruin the art underneath. It could also cause indentations in the face of the art work, which could show up as shadows when photographed. The flap is a handy place to record information such as the name of the project, the date, number of copies printed, and initials of anyone assuming responsibility for the proofreading (**proofreader**) and approval of the final copy.

You've Got a Friend
Instant and Commercial Printers

Both instant and commercial full-service print shops have a place in the graphics industry. Instant printers offer low cost, small quantities, and fast service, often in one day or less. Many instant print shops use paper plates on their presses which will give good quality on simple, short-run jobs. The disadvantages of this method are that it allows no room for improvement of the original copy, and it is generally limited to small quantities (less than 800 copies) because the paper plate does not hold up on longer runs. Because most instant print shops have limited equipment and small presses, they often prefer more simple designs and standard-sized paper; often they cannot exceed paper stock larger than 11 by 17 inches.

A full-service commercial print shop is able to offer high-quality, very complicated printing processes, and large quantities. Because of the more sophisticated equipment in commercial print shops they are able to take a concept and produce it from start to finish, maintaining color consistency and crisp definition, and they can provide halftones and four-color photographic images and binding services. The use of negatives and metal plates allows the commercial printer to improve on the original copy and run large quantities without sacrificing quality.

Most commercial shops have art departments with designers on the staff and in-house binding equipment, which allows complete control of printing and binding orders. Many also have the ability to do large mailings from customized mailing lists.

Working with a Cameraman or Printer

When working with a printing firm be clear and concise about what is wanted, or costly mistakes may occur. Convey information to the printer in one of the two methods below:

1. Attach a tag to the art work and give specific instructions for handling any reductions or enlargements, or advising of special techniques that are required.

2. Produce a **mock-up** (a model of the project with text and art in place) of the piece using a photocopier, sketches, etc., that will help the printer to visualize what is wanted. If you prepared a layout of the project before you proceeded with the art work and text, you can present that to the printer to help clarify what you want done.

Printers are professionals. Ask them for advice whenever information is needed about size, weight, cost, paper stock, or other technical questions that may occur as the project develops.

Page Proofs & What to Check For

When you send a project to the printer it will come back for approval as **page proofs** (copies of all pages of the project to be checked for errors, either of interpretation of your instructions to the printer, or something you may have left out when you prepared the camera-ready copy). These proofs should be carefully checked against your layout to make certain there are no errors.

If you are printing multiple pages, make sure all the pages are in correct order. Are the page numbers in place? Check for dust spots, uneven color, and spots of white on solid blocks of inked copy. If you are using photographs, are they sharp and clear, or fuzzy? Is the color true to the original? If you are printing letters or a graphic in white on a solid black or colored background (a "reverse"), check for little white spots on the solid color and be sure the edges of the letters or graphic are sharp and clear. If the piece is to be folded, do the ends meet correctly and is the crease sharp and clean?

Check the leading and line endings to be sure that the printer has not inadvertently chopped off any copy. Check horizontal and vertical alignment, and make sure there are no broken letters (letters which have not been fully printed). In short, make sure that all your instructions were followed. Some minor corrections or modifications may be necessary in any job. These corrections are divided into two categories at this stage: printer's errors and changes made by you. The cost of changes that you introduce at proof stage will be charged to you!

When all the changes and corrections have been clearly identified, the proof is returned to the printer. At this stage your project should be perfect, so if you have any doubts or questions, consult with your printer immediately before approving the proof for final printing.

Printing Costs & Material Specifications

To estimate the cost of printing, the printer needs an accurate idea of the work the project will require. A mock-up and list of material specifications (see page 42) should be supplied to several printers for estimating. Create the mock-up using the actual paper stock chosen for the project for a clear idea of what it will look like when finished. A mock-up is an excellent tool to use as a starting point for discussions about the technical specifications for the project, such as "What size will the page be?" "What weight of paper will be used?" "How many copies are needed?" "Will the project have a cover?" "Will it be printed with colored ink?"

A sample price list for printing is shown on page 42. Based on this list, printing 100 copies in black ink of a one-sided 8½-by-11-inch page would cost $6.70. One hundred copies printed in black ink of a two-sided project would cost $12.25. Using colored inks is a real temptation, but the cost can be prohibitive. The chart below illustrates just how expensive color work is: one additional color on one side of an 8½-by-11-inch sheet adds $22.00 to the cost! Screens (shading) can be an effective alternative to an additional color and are less expensive (see page 17 for examples of screens and background textures that may enhance your project inexpensively). The cost of a 4½-by-5½-inch screen is about $9.00; an 8½-by-11-inch screen costs $15.00. The more copies you print the less it costs per piece, so if you are considering multi-color work, the print run should be carefully considered.

MATERIAL SPECIFICATIONS AND
DELIVERY INSTRUCTIONS

Date: _____

Title of project: _____

Finished size: _____

Number of pages: _____

Quantity to print: _____

Ink color(s):
   Text: _____
   Cover: _____

Paper stock:
   Text: _____ lb. (weight)
   Color(s): _____

   Cover: _____ lb. (weight)
   Color(s): _____

Photographs:
   Number: _____
   Special effects required: _____
   Reductions required: _____
   Enlargements required: _____

Page proofs:
   Required: _____
   Not required: _____
   To attention of: _____

Binding requirements:
   Folded: _____
   Stapled: _____
   Saddle stitched: _____
   Plastic comb: _____
   Perforated: _____
   Laminated: _____

Delivery date: _____

Packing instructions: _____

Ship to: _____
_____

PRINTING COSTS

No. of copies	Black ink 8½x11, 20 lb. white 1 side	Black ink 8½x11, 20 lb. white 2 sides	Black ink 8½x14, 20 lb. white 1 side	Black ink 8½x14, 20 lb. white 2 sides	8½x11, 1 side 1 addl. color	8½x11, 1 side 2nd addl. color
100	6.70	12.25	9.15	15.95	28.70	56.25
500	16.95	27.45	21.50	36.00	38.95	71.45
1000	29.75	47.40	37.25	63.65	51.75	91.40
ea. addl. 1000	22.90	37.25	27.80	49.00	44.90	81.25

Keeping Your Act Together
Simple Binding Techniques

Some basic methods of binding (assembling) material together are described below.

Stapled. The top lefthand corner is the usual place for the staple. If you print more than three pages it might be wise to consider designing the piece with an interesting fold and avoid stapling altogether (see page 28 for various ways of folding a sheet).

Saddle stitched. The material is stapled through the fold of the spine. It is very inexpensive compared to other binding methods and allows the pages to lie flat when opened.

Plastic comb. An opening is drilled through the face of a stack of sheets and a comb is inserted to hold the pages together. This method is frequently used for cookbooks, notebooks, reports, and other materials that must lie perfectly flat when opened, for easy use. Material to be comb bound must have very deep **gutter** (the area surrounding the printed material, either between two facing pages or around the entire piece) margins to accommodate the binding; additional planning at the initial stage of development of the project is necessary.

Perforating. If a part of the page is to be detached, it could be perforated. This is done by the bindery after the piece is printed. The decision to include perforation in the original design should be carefully thought out. It costs about $15.00 to perforate 1,000 "tear-offs" on an 8½-by-11-inch sheet. Perforation is used for order forms or other material that you want returned. There are postal requirements for the weight of any piece that is to be mailed back. Before you decide to perforate anything, check with your local post office to be sure you are selecting the proper weight paper stock to meet all their regulations.

Laminating. You are probably already familiar with laminating materials for classroom use. The process consists of applying a layer of clear plastic material, such as mylar, to the face of the project, using heat. Lamination makes the colors sparkle and gives the project greater durability.

Thank You, Xerox
Using Your Photocopier as a Graphic Tool

Using a photocopier is a lot cheaper for reproducing small quantities than going to a printer, and you can take advantage of a variety of colored paper stocks. Some photocopiers produce clean line art; others are better for large dark areas. If you need to use a photocopier to produce your flyers or newsletter, try to find one in your community that produces the best possible quality reproduction. Be aware, however, that most do *not* reproduce photographs well!

A few materials are needed to transform photocopies into attractive finished items: a ruler or T-square for clean lines and perfect corners; scissors or an X-Acto knife for trimming; rubber cement or clear paste for mounting; and felt-tip pens and colored markers for brightening up your art. If you do not have a work surface with a mar-proof top, protect your work area with heavy cardboard. Always use paste in moderation to avoid lumpy areas. Some copiers will enlarge and reduce images in exact 1 percent increments; however, you should be aware that when you make a copy of a copy on most copiers, the quality of the image deteriorates very rapidly. If you have different types of copiers at your disposal, so much the better, because different brands will produce darker and more detailed copies. Experiment—trial and error is the best way to ensure that you are getting the best copy possible. Many photocopiers can also copy on gum-backed paper, which makes the production of attractive labels simple.

Always attach your project to the work surface with masking tape in the corners to keep it from moving around while you are working on it. To prevent smudging your copy when using colored pens or markers, lay a piece of paper under your hand (see also "Hang It Up," page 45 for a discussion of poster craft, the techniques of which also relate to using your photocopier successfully when producing art work).

Shadow lines may appear when an image has been pasted into position and then copied. Use white correction fluid to paint out any shadows before you copy your original.

Hang It Up
Poster Craft

The main requirements of a poster are to attract attention and to deliver a message. To do this, the poster must capture the viewer's attention immediately. Since every poster delivers a message, the visual elements can be as creative as the imagination will allow.

Theme Elements

List the illustrative elements that symbolize the desired message. Of the elements chosen, focus on just one or two words that will be the heart of the poster. All other elements of the poster will relate to these items.

Thumbnail Sketches

Make lots of **thumbnail sketches** (very small, hastily done sketches) using the elements selected to see how they flow together. The major words should be very large. Check the composition to see if it is balanced and has real impact. Don't crowd the lettering; isolated words can get a lot of attention, so concentrate on size, placement, and possible colors.

Poster proportions are generally 14 by 18 inches or so, but make many small sketches and scale them up later if necessary. When the final sketch is selected for enlarging, apply some color and check it for dramatic effect. If the sketch looks good small, it should look good enlarged also.

Materials Required

Before actually putting the poster together, assemble the materials needed:

Heavyweight paperboard, illustration board, or index card stock
Masking tape
Crayons, colored ink, pens, markers
Pencils
T-square, triangle, ruler

A T-square and triangle are needed for drawing guidelines for letter placement and for getting the project squared up. Tape the project down before working on it, and proceed with caution. If the sketch needs to be scaled up, refer to pages 34-35.

Technique

Transfer the final sketch in detail to the illustration board with very lightly drawn pencil lines, which can be erased later. Block in areas where color will go and where lettering will be, and indicate any large areas that will be solidly colored. Using colored markers, begin laying in the color for the background. In addition to regular markers, tips are available in ½-inch, 1-inch, and even 2-inch sizes for broad stroking, which is ideal for background areas. **Index card** stock is recommended when using markers since it is very smooth and will not allow ink to feather or spread at the edges. Be sure to replace caps on markers right after use, since they dry up rapidly.

If a white margin is required around the poster, place paper masking tape carefully along the edges. If colors overlap on the tape the poster won't be ruined. Use very thin paper tape and press the edges flat to avoid having ink run under them.

By studying travel posters, bookstore poster art, and all forms of advertising art, anyone can see the unlimited range of subjects that lend themselves to poster craft.

PART 2
Clip Art

VERY SIMPLE PROJECTS

- bookmarks
- children's activities
- invitations
- newsletters
- posters
- response coupons
- stationery and business cards

East Branch Library Presents
CHILDREN'S STORY HOUR

Every Tuesday 9:30 to 11:00

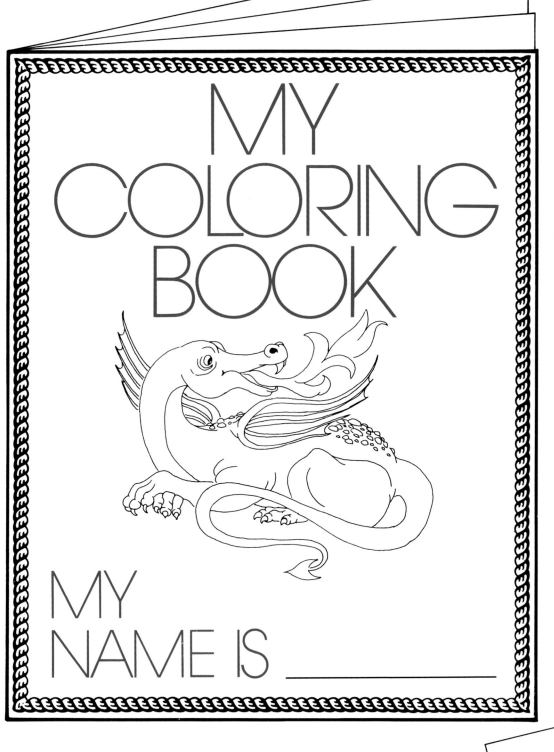

MY
COLORING
BOOK

MY
NAME IS _____

SUMMER LEISURE READING

Around Town

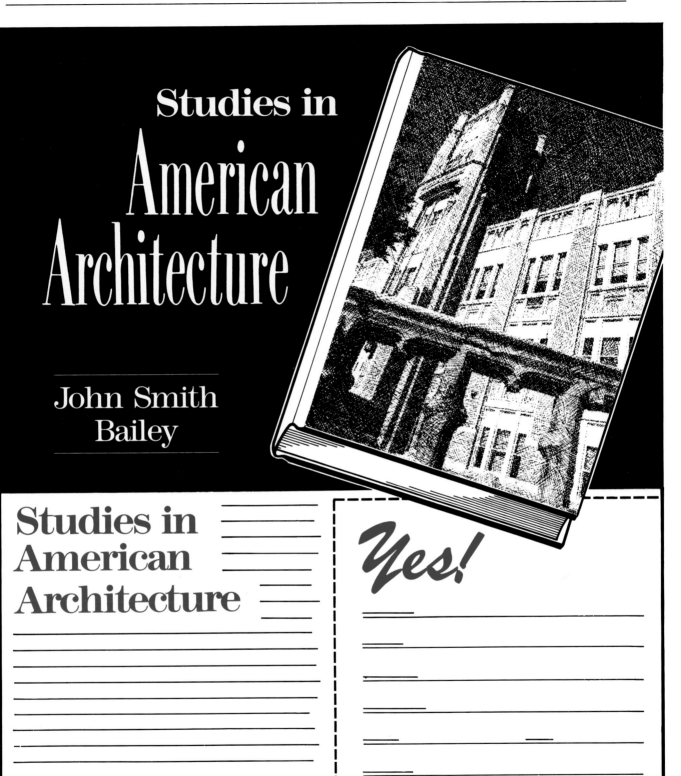

Studies in
American
Architecture

John Smith
Bailey

Studies in
American
Architecture

John Smith
Bailey

Yes!

BLACK HISTORY MONTH

February

All

Things

Bright &

Beautiful

Hamlet's Experience Simply Could Not Have Happened To A Plumber

WINTER

SUMMER

FALL

Spring

BE
A
FRIEND
OF
THE
LIBRARY

GET INVOLVED!
After School Sports

No Garden is Complete Without a Toad!

BOOKS, MORE BOOKS, & STILL MORE BOOKS

- books and computers
- books and globes
- books on shelves
- book spines
- closed books
- open books
- stacks of books

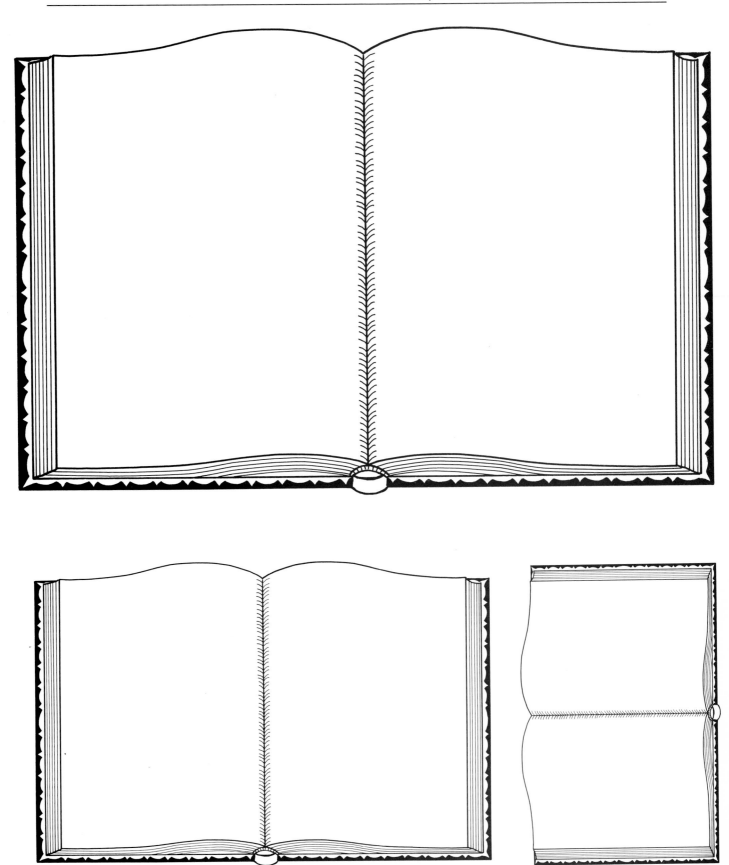

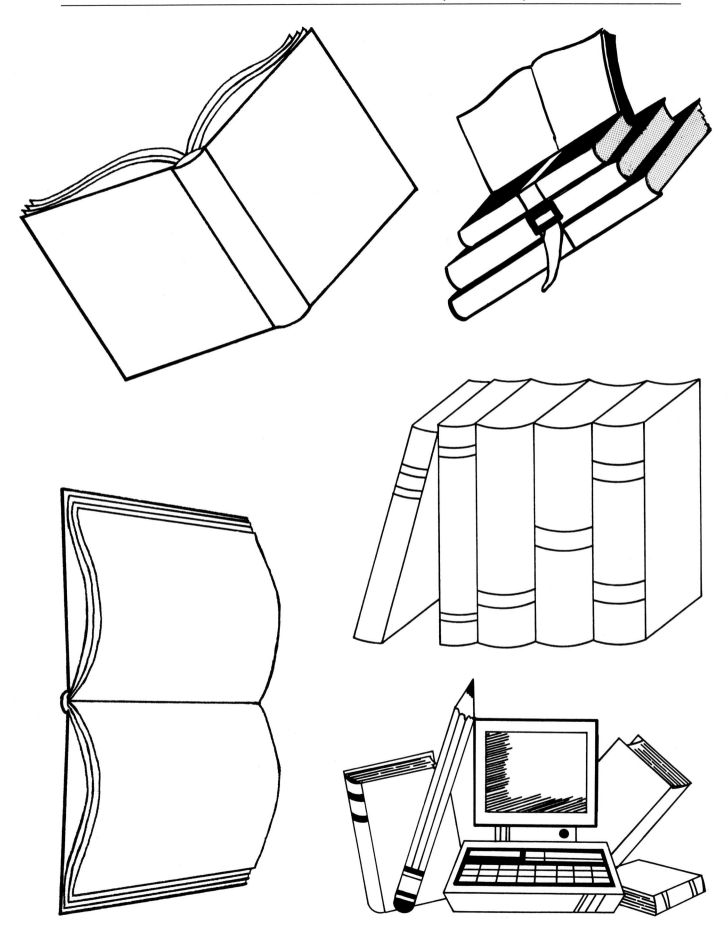

April showers bring May books!

DOING IT IN THE LIBRARY

- announcements
- book genres
- bookmarks
- bookmobiles
- bookplates
- types of libraries

PUBLIC

Visit Your LIBRARY!

Get All the ANSWERS at Your LIBRARY!

LEGAL

TECHNICAL

ACADEMIC

MEDICAL

SCHOOL

ADVENTURE

BIOGRAPHY

HISTORY

MYTHOLOGY

SCIENCE

GEOGRAPHY

SCI-FI

THE ARTS

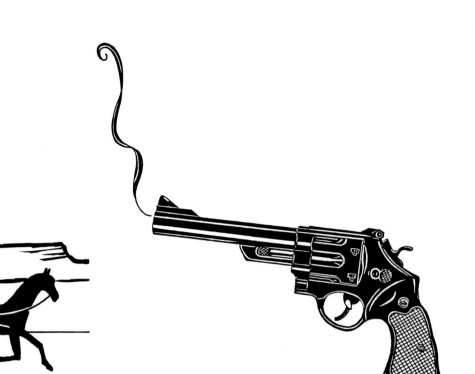

WESTERN

MYSTERY

FANTASY

ROMANCE

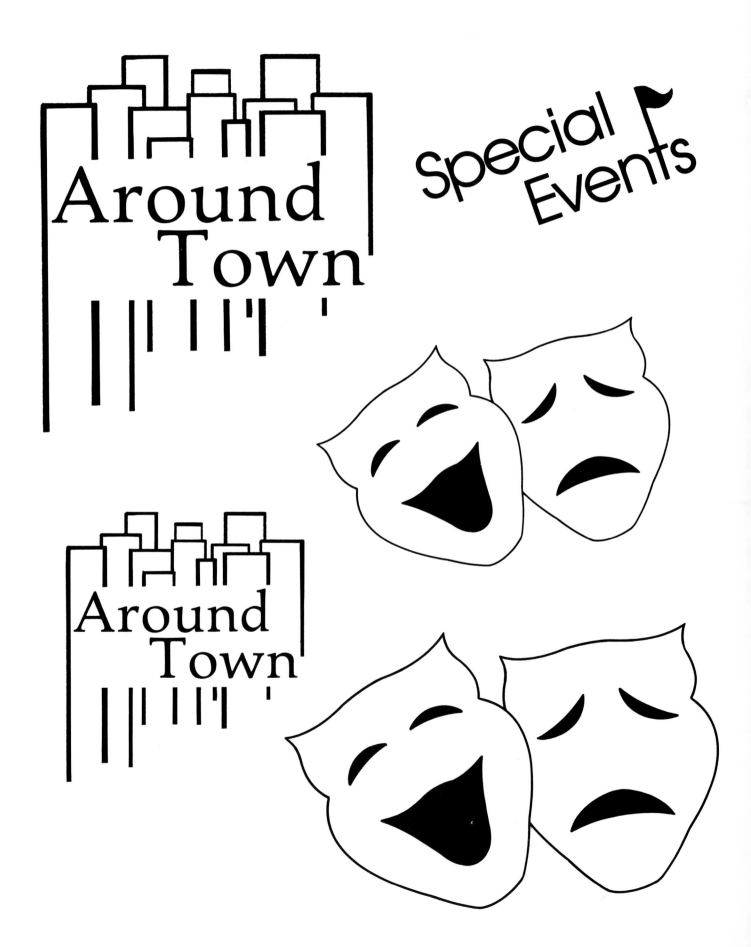

·MY BOOK·

at the LIBRARY

HAPPENINGS

CURIOUS?

Ask Your Librarian

QUIET

Back to School

Holidays & Monthly Potpourri

- birthdays
- Christmas
- "Color Me" pictures
- Easter
- elections
- Halloween
- Hanukkah
- important days, weeks, months
- monthly names and symbols
- patriotic symbols
- seasons and symbols
- St. Patrick's Day
- Thanksgiving
- Valentine's Day

JANUARY

FEBRUARY

MARCH

APRIL

MAY

JUNE

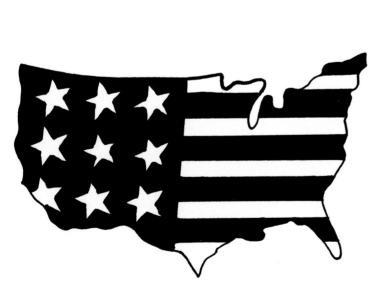

JULY

AUGUST

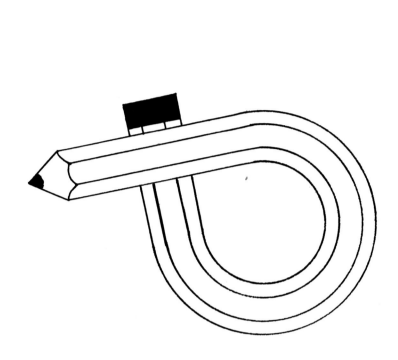

SEPTEMBER

OCTOBER

NOVEMBER

DECEMBER

January
February
March
April
May
June
July
August
September
October
November
December

January
February
March
April
May
June
July
August
September
October
November
December

January
February
March
April
May
June
July
August
September
October
November
December

January

Martin Luther King, Jr., Day
New Year's Day
National Hobby Month

February

Black History Month
American History Month
National Freedom Day
Valentine's Day
Washington's Birthday
Lincoln's Birthday
Groundhog Day

March

Mardi Gras
Red Cross Month
National Women's History Week
World Day of Poetry and Childhood
St. Patrick's Day

April

Easter
April Fools' Day
Passover
Pets Are Wonderful Month
National Coin Week
International Children's Book Day
Arbor Day
National Library Week

May

May Day
National Animal Health Week
Cinco de Mayo
Mother's Day
Armed Forces Day
Memorial Day
Victoria Day

June

Flag Day
Dairy Month
National Theatre Week
World Environment Day
Children's Day
Father's Day

July

Independence Day
Canada Day
National Ice Cream Month
Space Week
Bastille Day
4th of July

August

National Clown Week
Family Day
National Aviation Day
Women's Equality Day

September

Labor Day
International Literacy Day
National Grandparents' Day
American Newspaper Week
Banned Books Week
World Peace Day
Citizenship Day
International Day of Peace
Native American Day
Constitution Week

October
Halloween
Columbus Day
Fire Prevention Week
Child Health Day
Universal Children's Day
United Nations Day
National Unicef Day

November
Thanksgiving
Veterans Day
World Community Day
Aviation History Month
National Children's Book Week

December
Christmas
Hanukkah
Human Rights Week
Seasons' Greetings

 Spring

 SUMMER

 FALL

 WINTER

SPRING

SUMMER

FALL

WINTER

Happy Halloooooooween!

Spooky Tales

Spooks, Goblins, and MORE .... visit the Library on Halloween!

party animals

- animal silhouettes
- animals with books
- bookworm
- the classics
- leisure reading
- "Newton"
- reference desk
- story hour
- "teacher"
- term paper

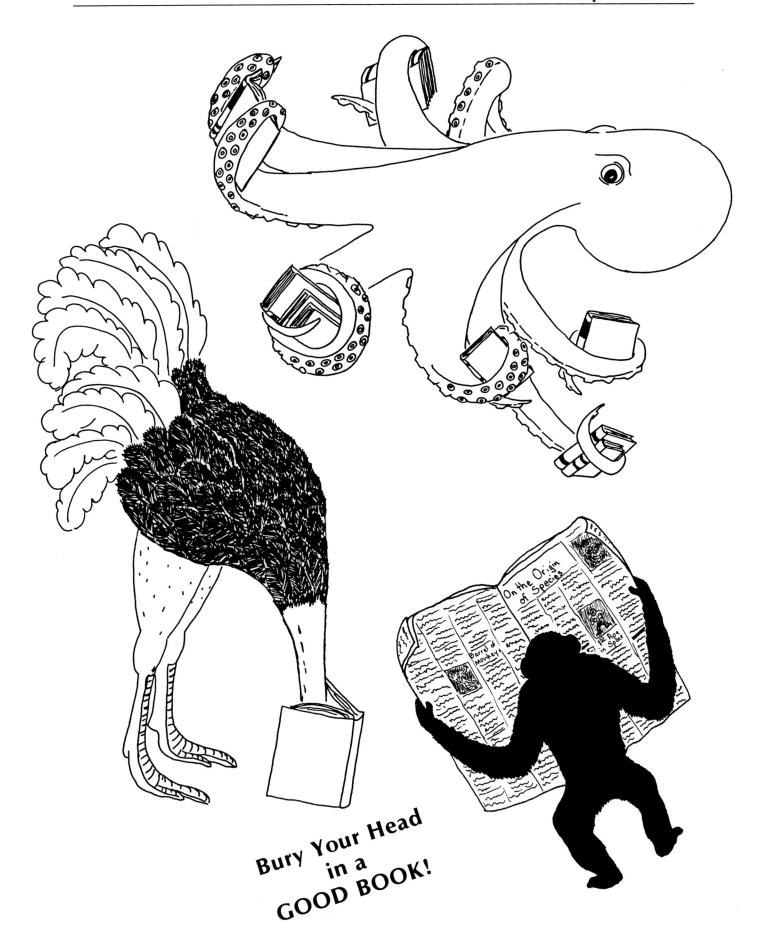

Bury Your Head in a GOOD BOOK!

Need help with your term project?
SEE THE LIBRARIAN

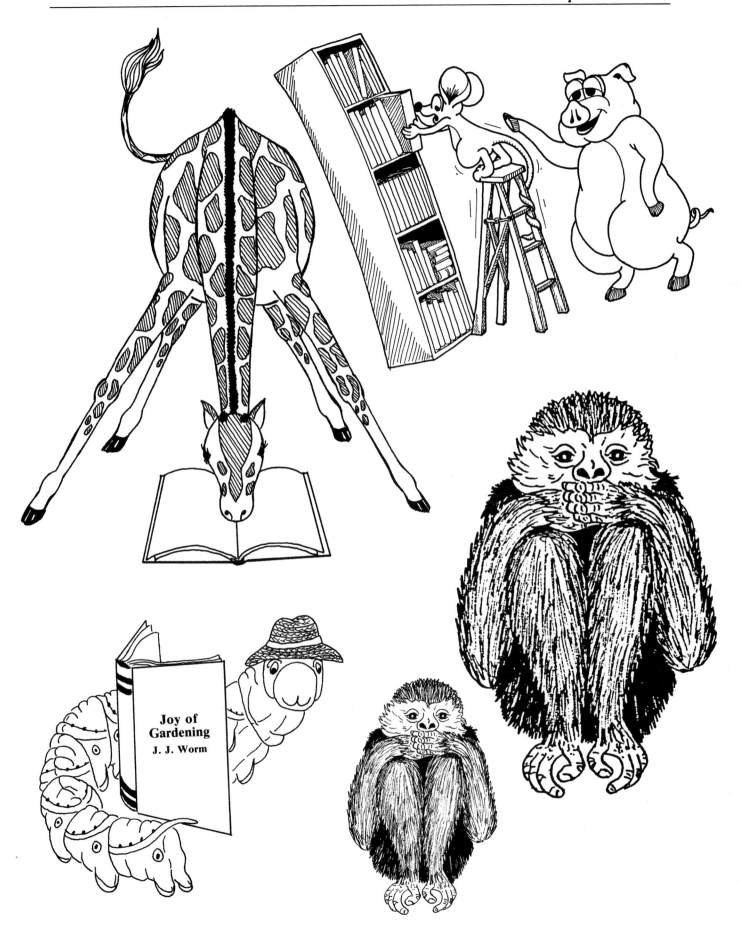

Joy of
Gardening
J. J. Worm

Hear Ye,
Hear Ye.

OUT IN THE OPEN

- ballooning
- birds
- "Color Me" ice cream cone
- "Color Me" leaves
- "Color Me" mushrooms
- horseback riding
- jogging
- summer sports
- winter sports

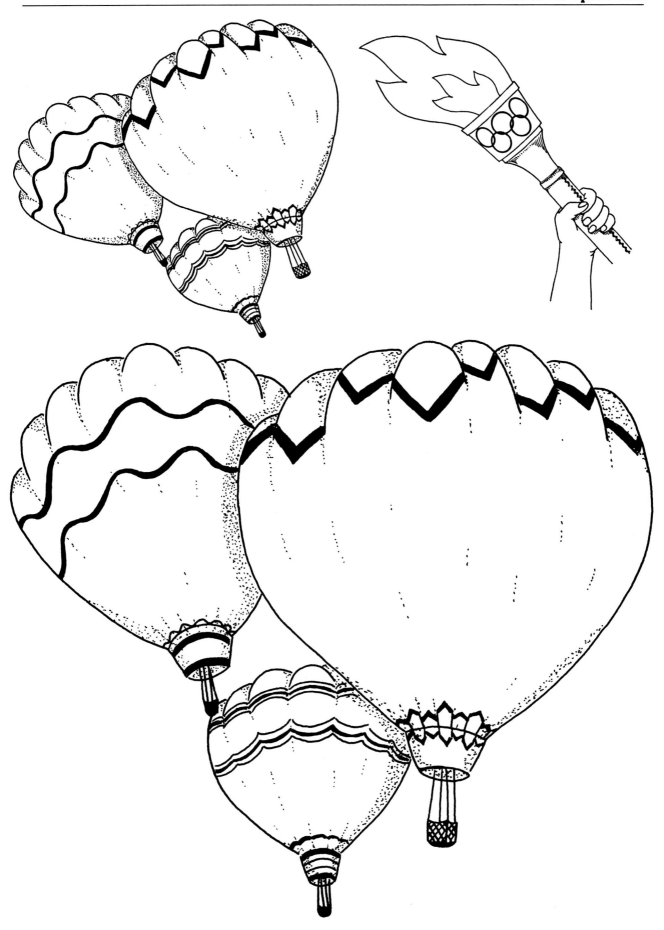

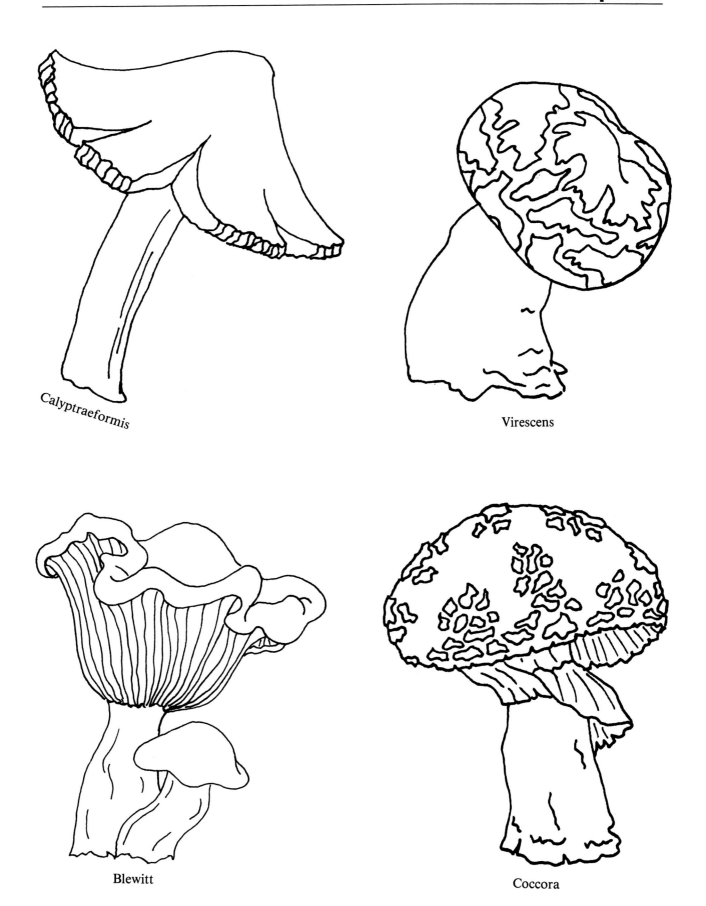

Calyptraeformis

Virescens

Blewitt

Coccora

Storybook Characters & Fancy Creatures

- "Color Me" teddy bears
- clowns
- dinosaurs
- dragons
- elves
- fairies
- Jack and the Beanstalk
- knights
- pirates
- prince, princess, and castle
- Red Riding Hood and the wolf
- Three Little Pigs
- unicorn and Pegasus
- witch

pretty boxes

- awards
- decorative borders
- scrolls

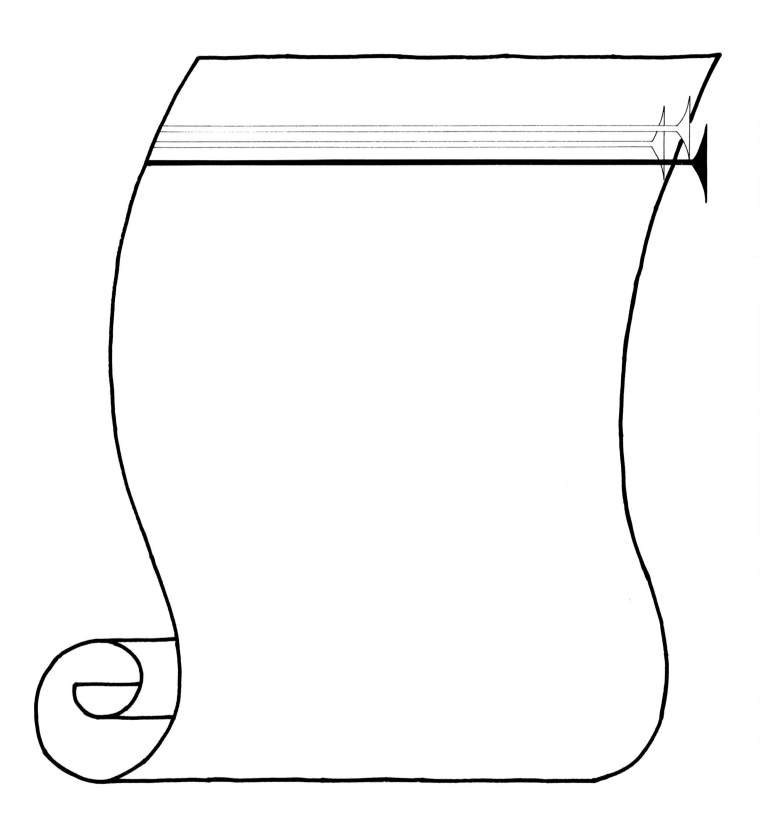

MESA
Public Library

John Doe

These borders were created with border tape. A full page example of each border is on the page indicated.

See page 49.

See page 60.

See page 69.

See page 80.

See page 104.

See page 118.

See page 128.

See page 140.

See page 153.

See page 157.

See page 166.

See page 172.

See page 176.

ATTENTION GETTING
DOO-DADS

- arrows
- banners
- cartoons
- exclamation points
- flowers
- headlines
- question marks
- sunbursts

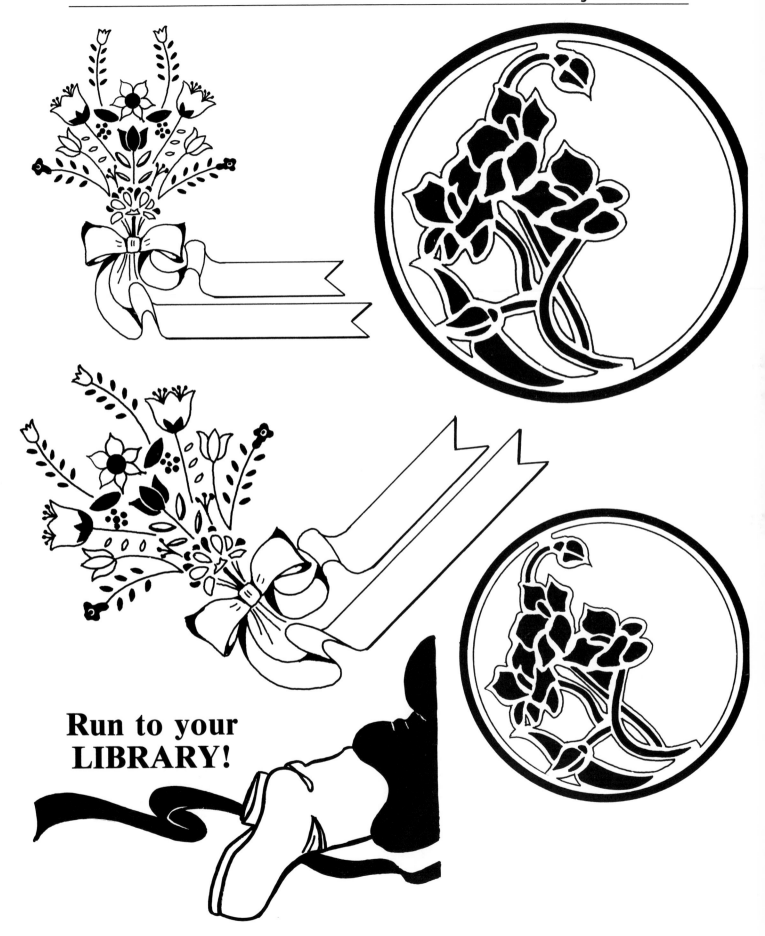

Run to your LIBRARY!

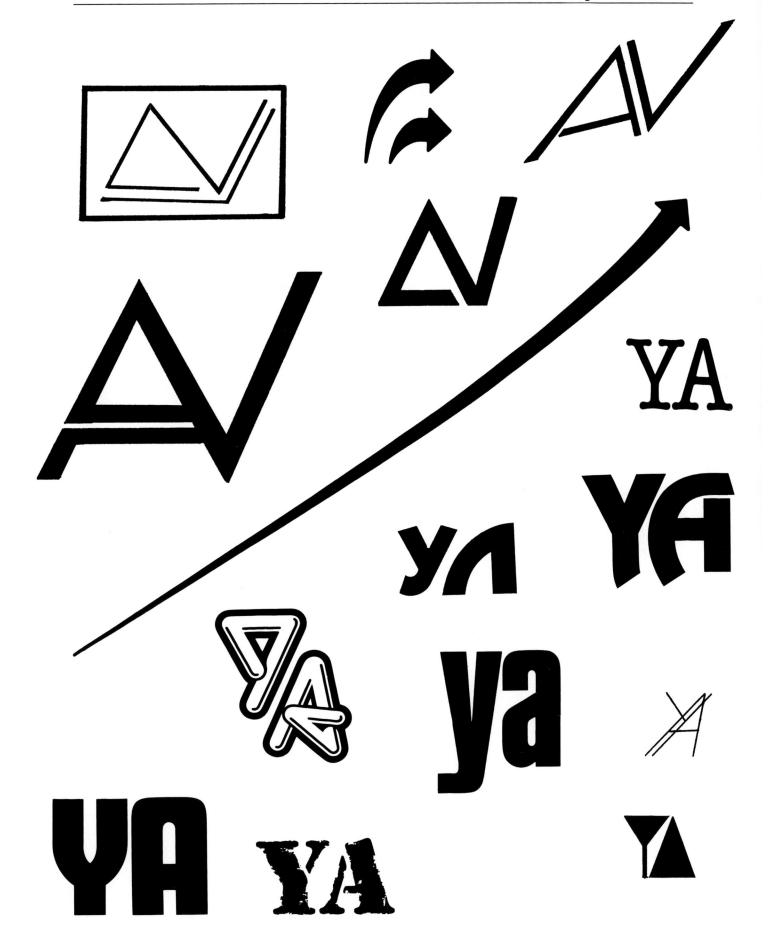

NEW! NEW! NEW!!

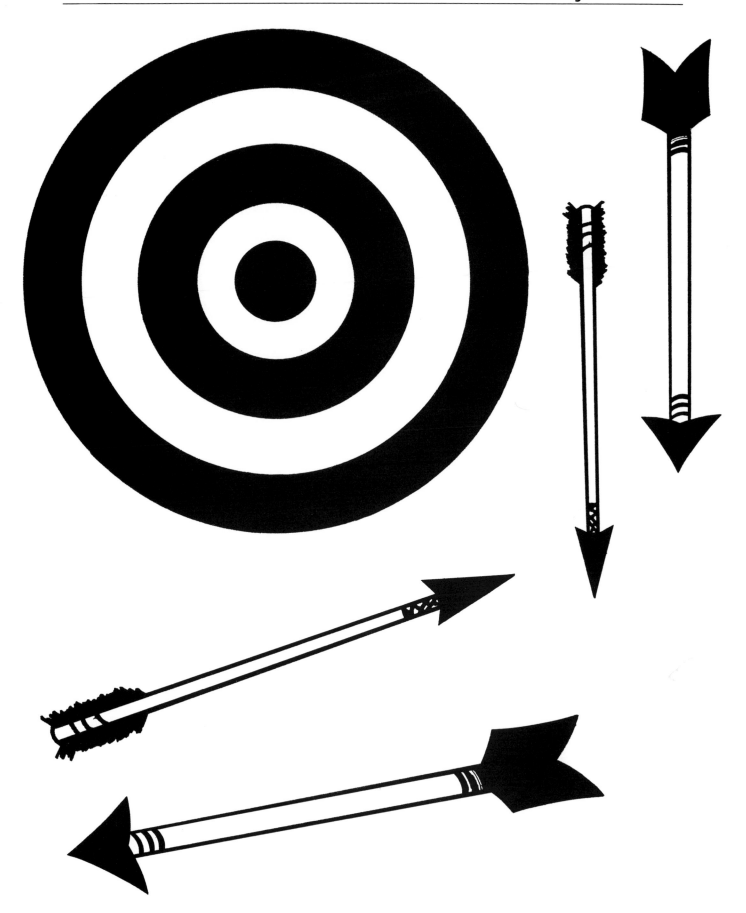

YOU OUGHTA BE IN PICTURES

- photographs of books
- photographs of schools
- special photographic effects

The photographs on these pages were taken with an ordinary 35mm camera by two of the authors, one of whom has no experience in photography whatsoever. Absolutely anyone can take pictures like these and then take them to a studio for the special effects.

These effects, which can be very dramatic, were done in a small camera studio. The best way to find one of these places, as they usually are NOT in the telephone directory, is to ask your printer. Costs are quite reasonable: the small photographs were about $10.00 each; the large, full page one was quite a bit more: $40.00.

You should be able to take a photograph of your school or library, or even a town building, and dress it up (even use it as a screen under your printing) to make your printed piece look very professional.

100 Line Halftone Screen

Line Shot

Straight-Line (coarse)

Concentric Circle

Steel Etched

Mezzotint (coarse)

MAPS & GRIDS

- half-inch grid
- quarter-inch grid
- United States map
- world map

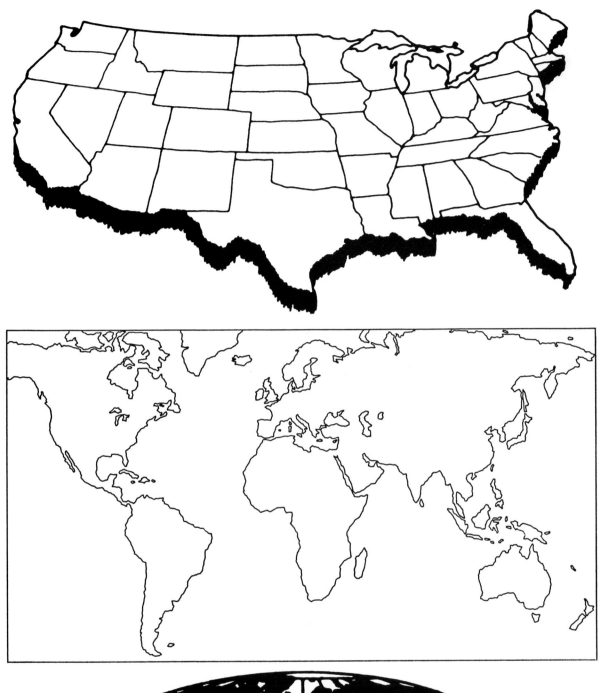

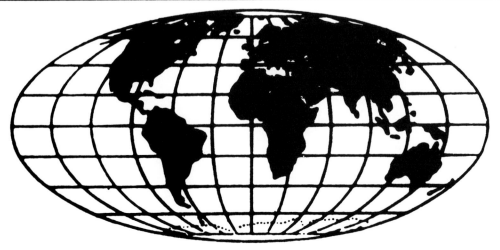

HEADLINES

- events
- library directives and phrases
- literary subjects

Do-It-Yourself
Bestsellers
Poetry
Romance
Current Events
Biography
Genealogy
Cook Books
Special Collections
Pets
New from Your Library
Consumer Information
Seniors

Book Sale
Fantasy
History
Mystery
Literature
Languages
Gardening
College Studies
VCRs
Sports
Movies
Photography

How to Use the Library

Accounting   Term Paper Information

Child Abuse   Thrillers
Computer Science   Sci-Fi
Travel   Lecture Series
Business Publications   Parenting
Job Seekers   The Classics
Tax Information   Crafts

HAPPENINGS

Story Hour

Summer Reading

National Library

Week

How to Use the Library

National Children's

Book Week

Back to School

CHECK THIS OUT

HAPPENINGS OF THE WEEK

TELEPHONE REFERENCE SERVICE

BESTSELLERS

MARK YOUR CALENDAR

MARK YOUR CALENDAR

AUTOMATION

BESTSELLERS

AUTOMATION

TELEPHONE REFERENCE SERVICE

HAPPENINGS OF THE WEEK

CHECK THIS OUT

SALE

NEWSLETTER

NEWSLETTER

NEWSLETTER

NEWSLETTER

REMINDER

BULLETIN

Story Hour

SALE

SALE

Bibliography

ALA Library Clip Art. Chicago: American Library Association, 1983.
   The format of this publication is a three-ring binder and the art is done on slick paper stock that has a backing that peels off and will stick to almost any surface. Some of the graphics are very strong and will suit many situations.

Biggles, Barry. *The Copy Catalogue*. New York: Pantheon Books/Random House, 1981.
   Party invitations, labels, catchy phrases, and attention-getters.

Bockus, H. William, Jr. *Advertising Graphics*, 4th edition. New York: Macmillan, 1986.

Clipper Creative Art Service. Peoria, Ill.: Dynamic Graphics, Inc. Monthly.
   This is the standard clip art service used by graphic artists and designers all over the continent. Very expensive, and extremely well-executed, but does not contain much for libraries.

Dover Publications, Inc. *Dover Clip Art Series*. New York.
   Very inexpensive. The art is copyright-free for the most part. Contains such titles as:
   Humorous Spot Illustrations
   Illustrations for Holidays and Special Occasions
   Illustrations of Children
   News Announcements
   Small Frames and Borders
   Sports Illustrations

Hart, Harold. *The Illustrator's Handbook*. New York: A & W Visual Library, 1978.

Ludlow, Norman H., Jr. *Clip Book* (various numbers). Rochester, N.Y.: N. H. Ludlow. (516 Arnett Blvd., Rochester, NY 14619).
   Includes various titles, such as:
   Action People Artwork
   Active Recreation Artwork
   People and Things We Live With

Missouri Library Association. Children's Services Round Table. *Clip to Go: Clip Art for Librarians*. Columbia, Mo.: Missouri Library Association, 1983.
   Lots of animal pictures, and a few book-oriented pictures. Some cute cartoons and hints for using material.

Ubinas, Dave, and Esther Langholtz. *Pick-up Book of Cartoon Style Illustrations*. New York: ARCO, 1979.

Watson, Sherry Lynn. *Snip and Snicker*. Wheat Ridge, Colo.: Central Colorado Library System, [1985].
Some humorous ideas and some excellent cartooning. A lot of the art is too busy to use as clip art. Makes delightful reading, however.

Glossary

Art: In general, all nontext material.

Art gum eraser: Nonabrasive all-purpose eraser used on all art projects.

Art mechanical: *See Mechanical.*

Ascender: That part of a lowercase letter that rises up from the body of the letter.

Baseline: An imaginary line that all letters and punctuation are aligned on.

Binder's Board: Heavy cardboard used for book covers.

Bleed: When copy, lines, or illustrations extend beyond the trim edge of a page. Also, when pens or markers feather around the edges.

Blueline proof: A proof copy of each page of the project received from the printer. All type and art appear blue. The proof is made from the negatives. Changes made after negatives are shot are very expensive.

Bold: Printing made to appear darker and more pronounced than regular letters.

Bone folder: A strip made of hard bone or plastic used for folding and creasing paper. *See also* Burnisher.

Burnisher: A device (similar to a pencil) made of plastic, animal bone, or metal, used to help transfer and smooth the edges of rub-on instant lettering.

Camera-ready: Material that is ready to be printed, with all elements pasted into position. *See also* Mechanical.

Caps: Short for all capital letters.

Clip art: Any art or design already created that can be cut out and used, with or without modification, to enhance the written word.

Color key: A type of proof that prints each color of the project on separate acetate layers so that exact positioning can be checked.

Comp: Short for comprehensive layout. An accurate mock-up of the final product showing head-lines, blocks of text, and illustrations, all in the correct size and position.

Condensed type: A "squeezed up" version of regular type that takes less space in a line than an equal number of letters of standard size.

Continuous tone: A photographic image that has grays or shades of color. Images with shades of gray must be broken up into a dot pattern to reproduce well, a process called screening. *See also* Halftone.

Crop: To select a part of an image by cutting off part of it to fit a defined area.

Cut and paste: To select text and graphic elements from various sources and recombine them to create a unique piece.

Descender: That part of a lowercase letter that falls below the body, such as the tail of a "y."

Display type: Used to attract attention, as in headlines. Usually 18 points and larger. *See also* Headline.

Dummy: A model of a project, without a great deal of detail, made for planning purposes. *See also* Mock-up.

Extended type: A wider, stretched out version of the normal type spacing. Also called expanded type.

Face: In type, a collection of letters and characters in a given style.

Family: Variations on the same basic typeface, such as medium, italic, and bold.

Font: A complete set of the letters and characters in one typeface and size.

Four-color process: A technique used to print photographs in full, natural color. There are four colors involved: yellow, red, blue, and black, thus four-color process.

Gang-run: To run several jobs at one time for cost effectiveness.

Gutter: Any area surrounding the printed material, either between two facing pages or around the entire piece.

Halftone: The photographic technique of showing shades of intensity by using various sizes of dots. *See also* Screen.

Headline: Bold or display type used to draw the reader's attention. *See also* Display type.

Illustration board: Lightweight white cardboard on which to prepare mechanicals (e.g., Bristol board).

Index card: A type of lightweight white cardboard with a very fine smooth surface, ideal for all projects where ink is used.

Instant lettering: Preprinted sheets of letters, numbers, punctuation, and symbols that you cut out of a backing sheet or rub off an acetate sheet and apply to art projects.

Italic: A typeface that slants to the right.

Justify: To align text along a margin (left or right), or to spread type from edge to edge in a given measure.

Keyline: Line drawn around copy or illustrations, either to be printed (e.g., boxed copy), or as a guideline only.

Kneaded eraser: Made of pliable rubber, it can be molded to the hand and is ideal for cleaning up delicate areas of art work.

Laid: The surface texture on paper which appears to have fine lines running through it in both directions.

Laminating: A process of using heat to apply clear plastic material to the face of a project, which results in greater durability.

Layout: A diagram and instructions for typesetting and placement of illustrations.

Leading: The amount of space between lines of type.

Line art: Illustrations drawn in black and white only.

Mechanical: The complete original art and text ready for printing, with all the elements positioned on illustration board or paper. *See also* Camera-ready.

Medium: A typeface style popular for use with text because of its readability. Medium is sometimes referred to as "regular" or "standard" to distinguish it from italic or bold.

Mock-up: A model of the project with text and art in place. *See also* Layout.

Negative: White print on a black background.

Nonreproducing blue pencil: Blue lead pencil that does not photograph when photographic negatives are made.

Opacity: The quality of paper that helps prevent type from showing through from one side to the other.

Opaque: To paint out unwanted areas on text or illustrations with white paint or correction fluid.

Overlay: Transparent paper or acetate laid over art work to show layering of elements, or for protection.

Page proofs: Copies of all pages of the project to be checked for errors.

Paste up: Pasting all the design elements in their proper positions on the mechanical.

Perforation: Generally a dashed line punched through paper or cardboard that is torn off; often used for coupons or other material that is to be returned by mail.

Photomechanical transfer (PMT): A copy of original material on slick paper that retains most of the detail of the original. Used for positioning purposes and as camera-ready art.

Pica: A unit of measure equal to approximately 1/6 of an inch; 6 picas equal approximately 1 inch.

Pick-up eraser: Designed to be used to pick up bits of dried rubber cement.

Plastic comb: A comb device inserted through holes punched along a stack of sheets to keep them together. Used for cookbooks, notebooks, and other material that must lie perfectly flat when open.

Point: A unit of measure 1/72 of an inch; 12 points equal 1 pica.

Positive: Black print on a white background.

Proofreader: The person who is responsible for checking type and illustrations to be sure that they are the same as the original copy.

Proportion wheel: Consists of two sliding circles with inches marked off. Percentages of original art or text to be reduced or enlarged are determined by sliding the two circles from the original size to the desired size. A figure appears in the window and represents the percentage of enlargement or reduction necessary to reach the desired size.

Register marks: A device applied to the face of art work to ensure correct positioning in printing. A cross in a circle or "L" brackets are generally used.

Reverse: White print on a black background. Also called negative.

Rough sketch: Preliminary sketch showing only important areas of blocked text and illustrations, without details. *See also* Thumbnail sketch.

Saddle stitch: Staples that are driven through the fold of the spine, instead of through the corner of two or more flat sheets.

Sans serif: Type styles that do not have extra strokes on the ends of the characters (serifs).

Scale: To determine the desired final dimensions of material which is to be enlarged or reduced.

Screen: Fine dot pattern that results in various intensities of original color. Used for creating the appearance of more than one color from the original color at less expense. *See also* Halftone.

Serif: Cross-stroke or ornament at the end of the main strokes of a character.

Show-through. Printing on one side of a sheet that is visible as a shadow on the other.

Stencil: Cardboard or other material, such as metal or wood, cut out with letters or designs whose outlines are traced onto a surface.

Template: Cardboard or other material (similar to a stencil) perforated with letters, punctuation, and designs whose outlines are traced onto a surface. Templates generally have risers to keep them off the work surface to avoid smearing when using ink to trace characters.

Thumbnail sketch: Very small, hastily done sketch, to provide a rough idea of what something will look like. *See also* Rough sketch.

Trim size: The full dimensions of the finished project.

Typeface weight: Variations of letters and characters such as light, bold, extra bold, and italic.

Typography: The style, arrangement, and appearance of typeset material. In graphics, the art of combining different heights and weights of letters to produce pleasing type that is easy to read.

Word spacing: The space between words.

Woven: A surface texture on paper that has a uniform, smooth surface.

X-Acto knife: Lightweight, handheld knife used to trim around intricate art work.

X-height: The size of a lowercase "x," which is also the height of the lowercase letters excluding ascenders and descenders.

Index